MW00949425

Bride of Christ – Prepare Now!

by Susan Davis

© Copyright 2013 – Susan Davis

ISBN-13: 978-1490519029

ISBN-10: 1490519025

Unless indicated otherwise, all Scripture reference and notes are from the King James Version Bible.

TABLE OF CONTENTS

ABOUT THESE PROPHECIES

Susan operates in the gift of prophecy. In 1 Corinthians 14:1 it states, "Follow the way of love and eagerly desire gifts of the Spirit, especially prophecy." Now we are living and supposed to be obeying God's instructions in the New Testament. Although some believe that spiritual gifts, such as prophecies, have been done away with, this is man's thinking and not God's. God has not changed His covenant. We are still living in the era of the New Covenant – which is also called the New Testament. Please understand that your first commitment should be to the Lord Jesus Christ and His Word as written in the Bible – especially the New Testament.

As always, all prophecy needs to be tested against the Bible. However, if the prophecy lines up with the Bible then we are expected to obey it. Currently God does not use prophecies to introduce new doctrines. They are used to reinforce what God has already given to us in the Bible. God also uses them to give us individual warnings of future events that will affect us.

Just like in the Old Testament, God uses prophets in the New Testament times of which we are currently in. The book of Acts, which is in the New Testament, mentions some of the prophets such as Judas and Silas (Acts 15:32) and Agabus (Acts 21:21) and there were others. The ministry of prophets is also mentioned in New Testament times in 1 Corinthians 12:28, 14:1,29,32,37 as well as in Ephesians 2:20,3:5,4:11.

Jesus chooses prophets to work for Him on earth. Among other things, Jesus uses prophecies and prophets to communicate His desires to His children. The Bible itself was written prophetically through the inspiration of the Holy Spirit.

3

Some people say words of prophecy are in danger of adding to the Bible or taking from it -- well the Bible speaks of prophecy as being a Gift of the HOLY SPIRIT. The way the Bible is added to or taken from is not through additional words of prophecy received by the people which the HOLY SPIRIT gives words to, but by the changing of GOD's concepts to add new unBiblical concepts from other pagan beliefs for example. But the primary work of the prophets in the Bible has always been to focus the people back to GOD's WORD, the BIBLE.

As it says in 1 Thessalonians 5:19-21, "Do not put out the Spirit's fire; do not treat prophecies with contempt. Test everything. Hold on to the good." And the way to test the messages is to compare it's content to what the Bible says.

In all the prophecies below I personally (Mike Peralta - Book Preparer) have tested these messages and they are all in agreement to what the Bible says. But you must also test these messages, yourself, to the Bible. And if they are consistent with the Bible, then God expects that you will take them to heart and obey His instructions.

CHAPTER 1

Only Those Who Are FULLY Committed To ME

Will Feel Safe Now

Sat, 19 Jan 2013

The LORD's Words:

"Only Those Who Are FULLY Committed To ME Will Feel Safe Now."

The world is becoming increasingly darker: the politics; the things people call "entertainment"; the way people are indifferent and cold-hearted toward others; the rejection of GOD and moral leadership in all nations; the worldwide economic downward spiral; the embracing of humanistic / atheistic / paganistic / satanistic cultural views; the world's overall obvious leaning toward antichrist thinking and the rejection of the Will of GOD—to name a few...

Almost daily I receive letters from people who are troubled by a dark future outlook as well as a myriad of challenges people are facing in their personal lives. Most specifically—the bride of CHRIST and those truly seeking GOD are getting beat up by the enemy. LISTEN to me: you are not alone in your struggles. Don't think it strange that your life seems in a turmoil...LOT'S OF GOD'S PEOPLE ARE GETTING RAKED OVER THE COALS. The enemy is in his LAST hour and he wants to torment GOD's people and those who are turning away from darkness back to light.

I am writing about this because I don't want people to think they are running solo in this incredible war the enemy is waging on those who are truly seeking GOD in these closing moments before the

LORD returns and darkness completely envelopes the earth. HANG IN THERE—Cover yourself in the BLOOD of CHRIST—the BLOOD IS INVINCIBLE.

Not quite a year ago, the LORD led me to do a 40-day water fast in a secluded location. I thought it was only about dealing with personal issues at first (yes, the LORD did deal with my personal stuff)—however, I did not know that HE was planning to dictate to me a series of letters that would later become a powerful book that would warn many people about HIS soon coming and end times preparation. (The book is called the MARRIAGE SUPPER OF THE LAMB and you can get it free, downloaded here: https://www.smashwords.com/books/view/162979)

As I began to go through this fasting, I knew that the letters I received daily were very important to the LORD and I knew that I just had to make it through for the full 40 days. Into week four, with still another week to go was such a huge struggle. I looked in the mirror wondering if there would be anything left of me at the end and how this would upset my family and my son in particular. But I knew that GOD was with me and that I was probably in the safest place I could be—right where the LORD had called me to be. My family and friends really were concerned, but I just knew GOD would get me through it. The reason I am bringing this up is at my lowest point when I thought I could not make it through this thing—I thought to myself: "There must be a million people in hell who would trade places with me in this 40-day fast." That thought spurred me on. And now I am telling you—that no matter how rough your current situation is (not to make light of it) there are millions in hell who would trade places with you now. So, have courage—the LORD is with you if you are with HIM. Don't give up—don't stop praying for those around you. NEVER GIVE UP. (The LORD gave me this scripture for you now: Psalm 23:4, Yea, though I walk through the

6

valley of the shadow of death, I will fear no evil: for thou art with me; thy rod and thy staff they comfort me.)

Below the LORD's Letters are NEW visions from readers and an important message about the Mark of the Beast. At the very bottom of this letter is a list of the past letters from the LORD covering many important topics relevant to the times we are living in. Also below is an invitation to download and read the FREE Marriage Supper of the LAMB Ebook with Words from the LORD for this end time generation. THIS BOOK IS CHANGING LIVES! THE MP3 AUDIO VERSION of the Marriage Supper of the LAMB are now available in this letter plus links to Spanish Version of the book. Plus sign up to receive the hottest ever end times headlines coming across our desks in the End Times News Report we put out each week. Plus the latest words/visions from young brothers Jonathan and Sebastian and Buddy Baker. Also, to read past letters from the LORD you can visit this link:

http://end-times-prophecy.com/blog/?category_name=2012-the-lords-messages

Special Note:New links for Deborah Melissa Moller's book, "The Final Call" in Spanish—see below with the Final Call information.

Words of the LORD:

"It Is An Abomination To Believe The Plans Of Men Over Your God."

(Words Received from Our LORD by Susan, January 12, 2013)

I am ready to bring you Words:

Children, MY coming is nigh. I am warning but few are listening. They would rather listen to men speak about the future—this is evil apart from GOD—apart from MY Words, Truth. I have laid out MY Plans and the signs to watch for: instead you choose to watch what men believe the future holds. This is evil. It is an abomination to believe the plans of men over your GOD.

MY Word says to watch when you see all the signs I have given come to pass, yet you choose to believe lowly men who never pursue their GOD: WHO Knows what the future of men hold. Do they consult ME? Seek MY Face? Practice MY Ways? Read MY Word? Or do they listen to each other's evil schemes, even seeking the words of the dead and demonic. This is a tyranny to MY Kingdom. Evil is running high and wide across the land.

Few know MY Word and practice MY Ways. Few want Truth and prescribe to the Word of GOD. All that men need is laid out in MY Word. It is complete in its instruction for lost and floundering men. Anyone who wants to find ME can find ME in MY Word, but each must have a desire to press in and lay down the distractions of the world in exchange for the knowledge available in MY Teachings: through MY Word and the HOLY SPIRIT, WHO leads you in understanding MY Word. There is no other way. It is not through the understanding of men who they, themselves are apart from GOD. This is not how you will understand MY Word. All knowledge of MY Word can be pursued by those who have hungry hearts and surrender their lives, making ME FULL LORD and MASTER.

I am the ONE WHO Leads and Directs the way along the narrow path. Don't be deceived. All other teachings of men apart from MY SPIRIT will lead you astray down dark broad paths of destruction, eternal hell. Come into MY Light. Seek the Eternal Lamp and Oil of MY HOLY SPIRIT so that you will not lack saving knowledge.

MY coming is soon. MY coming is sure. Don't be found when I come without a full oil lamp. These are dark days. You need your lamp oil full. Many will scramble to know ME after I take out MY church. It will be a dark time for the church left behind. Choose now to avoid what is coming. If you disregard MY Warnings you will face the consequences of your decision. I must tell the Truth.

This is the LORD WHO Knows the Future...

Coordinating Scripture:

James 4:13-14, 13 Go to now, ye that say, Today or tomorrow we will go into such a city, and continue there a year, and buy and sell, and get gain: 14 Whereas ye know not what shall be on the morrow. For what is your life? It is even a vapour, that appeareth for a little time, and then vanisheth away.

Isaiah 31:1, Woe to them that go down to Egypt for help; and stay on horses, and trust in chariots, because they are many; and in horsemen, because they are very strong; but they look not unto the HOLY ONE of Israel, neither seek the LORD!

Deuteronomy 18:10-12, 10 There shall not be found among you any one that maketh his son or his daughter to pass through the fire, or that useth divination, or an observer of times, or an enchanter, or a witch. 11 Or a charmer, or a consulter with familiar spirits, or a wizard, or a necromancer. 12 For all that do these things are an abomination unto the LORD: and because of these abominations the LORD thy GOD doth drive them out from before thee.

1 Corinthians 2:13-14, 13 Which things also we speak, not in the words which man's wisdom teacheth, but which the HOLY GHOST teacheth; comparing SPIRITUAL things with SPIRITUAL. 14 But the

natural man receiveth not the things of the SPIRIT of GOD: for they are foolishness unto him: neither can he know them, because they are SPIRITUALLY discerned.

Hosea 4:6, MY people are destroyed for lack of knowledge: because thou hast rejected knowledge, I will also reject thee, that thou shalt be no priest to ME: seeing thou hast forgotten the law of thy GOD, I will also forget thy children.

Matthew 25:4, But the wise took oil in their vessels with their lamps.

Words of the LORD:

"Only Those Who Are FULLY Committed To ME Will Feel Safe Now."

(Words Received from Our LORD by Susan, January 14, 2013)

I will give you words for the people:

These are trying times for my people. The evil is enclosing them. There is evil at every turn. Even the safe places are getting dark.

Evil is even invading the places that should be safe. MY people, MY church, those I call MY bride: I want you to know I am with you. I know you feel like you are alone and there are very few that understand you. Do not fear. I am always with you no matter where you go. This is not the hour to be filled with fear.

You are MY people, MY true bride. I will not let the enemy come between us, if you give ME your ALL. Surrender your ALL and live in peace. This is where you can find peace, even in the storm.

The storm clouds are rolling in. Evil is now at every corner. Only those who are FULLY committed to ME will feel safe now: only those who keep their eye and focus on ME. Everyone else will live with the uneasiness of a world that is growing very dark with a future that looks very dark.

There is trouble brewing, make no mistake. Darkness is closing in. But these dark clouds do not have to be over you. I can release you from this overwhelming fear of the future, if you surrender your ALL to ME and trust ME with ALL your ways.

I am the Great EMANCIPATOR. I can free you from the plans of the enemy who wants to lead you and everyone around you into darkness, destruction, and death. I am a GOD ready to liberate, ready to protect, ready to bring you into safety, but you must desire this from ME. I cannot force you into this shelter, although MY Arms are safe and I am the SAFE ROUTE, the NARROW PATH. You must decide to follow ME.

Don't be dismayed. I do offer the light at the end of the tunnel. Follow ME to safety, a peace everlasting, a haven of rest, and safe keeping even in the darkest hour. I am a STRONG TOWER in dark times. Turn to ME before it is too late. Let me rescue you, be among MY church, MY bride. These Words are for your comfort in these difficult days.

This is your LORD, SAVIOR, and RESCUER.

Coordinating Scripture:

Proverbs 18:10, The Name of the LORD is a STRONG TOWER: the righteous runneth into it, and is safe.

1 John 4:18, There is no fear in love; but perfect love casteth out fear: because fear hath torment. He that feareth is not made perfect in love.

Luke 21:26, Men's hearts failing them for fear, and for looking after those things which are coming on the earth: for the powers of heaven shall be shaken.

CHAPTER 2

This Is MY Lukewarm Church: The Adulterous Flavor In MY Mouth Will Cause ME To Spit Her Out

Mon, 28 Jan 2013

The LORD's Words:

"This Is MY Lukewarm Church—The Adulterous Flavor In MY Mouth Will Cause ME To Spit Her Out."

When we look out beyond ourselves we can look to the LORD and find LIGHT. But imagine, GOD WHO is perfect, pure, righteous—when HE looks out beyond HIMSELF what does HE see if HE is the only source of LIGHT? This is why I believe it is so important to GOD for HIS creation to empty itself of "self" to make room for HIS LIGHT—the filling of the HOLY SPIRIT in the person who surrenders completely to make CHRIST LORD and MASTER. GOD looks out beyond HIMSELF and then sees a reflection of HIMSELF in HIS OWN creation and this must be very pleasing to HIM.

Have you surrendered your ALL to the LORD allowing HIM to fill you with HIS SPIRIT completely? You just have to repent of your sins and ask the LORD from a heart that truly desires to be in the perfect Will of GOD.

The BELOVED

(Scripture from King James Version)

Song of Solomon 5:10: My BELOVED is white and ruddy, the CHIEFEST AMONG TEN THOUSAND.

Luke 23:38: And a superscription also was written over HIM in letters of Greek, and Latin, and Hebrew, This Is The KING of the Jews.

Song of Solomon 5:11: HIS Head is as the most fine gold, HIS Locks are bushy, and black as a raven.

John 19:2: And the soldiers platted a crown of thorns, and put it on HIS Head, and they put on HIM a purple robe,

Song of Solomon 5:12: HIS Eyes are as the eyes of doves by the rivers of waters, washed with milk, and fitly set.

John 17:1: These words spake JESUS, and lifted up HIS Eyes to heaven, and said, FATHER, the hour is come; glorify THY SON, that THY SON also may glorify THEE:

Song of Solomon 5:13: HIS Cheeks are as a bed of spices, as sweet flowers:

Isaiah 50:6: I gave MY Back to the smiters, and MY Cheeks to them that plucked off the hair: I hid not MY Face from shame and spitting.

Song of Solomon 5:13: HIS Lips like lilies, dropping sweet smelling myrrh.

Isaiah 53:7: HE was oppressed, and HE was afflicted, yet HE opened not HIS Mouth: HE is brought as a lamb to the slaughter, and as a sheep before her shearers is dumb, so HE openeth not HIS Mouth.

Song of Solomon 5:14: HIS Hands are as gold rings set with the beryl:

John 20:27: Then saith HE to Thomas, Reach hither thy finger, and behold MY Hands;

Song of Solomon 5:14: HIS Belly is as bright ivory overlaid with sapphires.

John 20:27: and reach hither thy hand, and thrust it into MY Side: and be not faithless, but believing.

Song of Solomon 5:15: HIS Legs are as pillars of marble, set upon sockets of fine gold:

John 19:33: But when they came to JESUS, and saw that HE was dead already, they brake not HIS Legs:

Song of Solomon 5:15: HIS Countenance is as Lebanon, excellent as the cedars.

Isaiah 52:14: As many were astonished at THEE; HIS Visage was so marred more than any man, and HIS Form more than the sons of men:

Song of Solomon 5:16: HIS Mouth is most sweet: yea, HE is altogether lovely. This is MY BELOVED, and this is MY FRIEND, O daughters of Jerusalem.

Isaiah 53:9: And HE made HIS grave with the wicked, and with the rich in HIS Death; because HE had done no violence, neither was any deceit in HIS Mouth.

Below the LORD's Letters are NEW visions from readers and an important message about the Mark of the Beast. At the very bottom of this letter is a list of the past letters from the LORD covering many important topics relevant to the times we are living in. Also below is

an invitation to download and read the FREE Marriage Supper of the LAMB Ebook with Words from the LORD for this end time generation. THIS BOOK IS CHANGING LIVES! THE MP3 AUDIO VERSION of the Marriage Supper of the LAMB is now available in this letter plus links to Spanish Version of the book. Plus sign up to receive the hottest ever end times headlines coming across our desks in the End Times News Report we put out each week. Plus the latest words/visions from young brothers Jonathan and Sebastian and Buddy Baker. Also, to read past letters from the LORD you can visit this link: http://end-times-prophecy.com/blog/?category_name=2012-the-lords-messages
Special Note: New links for Deborah Melissa Moller's book, "The Final Call" in Spanish—see below with the Final Call information.

Words of the LORD:

"This Is MY Lukewarm Church—The Adulterous Flavor In MY Mouth Will Cause ME To Spit Her Out."

(Words Received from Our LORD by Susan, January 21, 2013)

Daughter let ME give the people new Words:

Children of the MOST HIGH:

The world is growing dim—the LIGHT is diminishing. All that is good and pure and holy is falling to the wayside. MY enemy is destroying all that is good and pure—and replacing it with evil and darkness. He is desensitizing the world to MY Righteousness and what is of most value: the HOLINESS of GOD.

The world is plummeting into deep darkness, outer darkness with its plans and thoughts apart from the ONE TRUE GOD. Soon the world will be dumbstruck when I remove MY church and all that remains is the horror of a world deplete of True Holiness and the Righteousness of GOD.

This nightmare is coming for those who refuse to come into MY Will and will be left behind. Their decision to reject ME now, MY Word, MY Leadership in their life, and their FULL surrender to ME will leave them facing the leadership, tyranny of the unholy alliance of satan, the antichrist, and their false prophet. This alliance will take in the world by demonic deception, leading the world down a blind alley of destruction to eternal hell—the location of the destination of MY enemy. He plans to take so many with him as he can pursue, control, and deceive. He will succeed—many will see destruction and fall into everlasting hell and torment.

The only way to stop him and his blood thirsty rampage will be MY Second Coming when I arrive to earth with MY holy army, MY church, to stop the mouth of the enemy with the Sword of MY Mouth; to chain up and cast him into hell until he is released one thousand years later. His ultimate end will be the Lake of Fire along with the vast majority of humanity that is taken over by the enemy's deception. This, because the people refuse to surrender their personal will to ME, follow the Teachings of MY HOLY SPIRIT by receiving HIS Baptism. Without the Baptism of MY HOLY SPIRIT which comes when MY children willingly surrender their all to ME, they are not ready when I come in Glory to receive MY church.

Asking for salvation is not the same thing. Many have received salvation but have not yet made ME their LORD and MASTER. This is MY lukewarm church—their relationship with ME is tepid and incomplete. I am not their "ALL IN ALL." They handle the Holy only partially along with the world and their partial relationship is like that of a whore who wants their LORD and MASTER a little but wants to go whoring with the world. I am not good enough to submit to in FULL relationship.

This is MY lukewarm church—the adulterous flavor in MY Mouth will cause ME to spit her out. I cannot take her out with ME to MY Holy Kingdom as she will not be a pure bride. Her hands are dirty handling the world every chance she gets with her eyes, her thoughts, her heart. I can't take it. I gave her ALL of ME and she wants to bring the world into our bed. She repulses ME. I am coming soon and I will leave her standing at the altar of her lukewarm churches wondering why her BRIDEGROOM left her behind. She will pine and be forlorn for ME then when she realizes what she has done and that she is left with a cruel lover who will demand her life.

This is what the lukewarm church will face. Come back to ME O' great church of the lukewarm followers. Come wash your garments in MY Blood. Lay your life down. Leave the world behind. Reject MY enemy and the hold he has over you. You are soon going to be left behind. MY coming is swift. Don't be foolish. Fill your oil lamps. Come get priceless oil from your LORD.

I drank of the cup and now I offer you pure oil from the same cup for your lamp. Let ME fill your cup so it runneth over.

This is your BRIDEGROOM

PURE—HOLY—RIGHTEOUS

Coordinating Scripture:

Philippians 2:15, That ye may be blameless and harmless, the sons of GOD, without rebuke, in the midst of a crooked and perverse nation, among whom ye shine as lights in the world;

Revelation 20:1-3, And I saw an angel come down from heaven, having the key of the bottomless pit and a great chain in his hand. 2 And he laid hold on the dragon, that old serpent, which is the devil, and satan, and bound him a thousand years, 3 And cast him into the bottomless pit, and shut him up, and set a seal upon him, that he should deceive the nations no more, till the thousand years should be fulfilled: and after that he must be loosed a little season.

Revelation 20:10, And the devil that deceived them was cast into the lake of fire and brimstone, where the beast and the false prophet are, and shall be tormented day and night forever and ever.

Revelation 2:16, Repent; or else I will come unto thee quickly, and will fight against them with the sword of MY Mouth.

Revelation 3:15-17, 15I know thy works, that thou art neither cold nor hot: I would thou wert cold or hot. 16So then because thou art lukewarm, and neither cold nor hot, I will spue thee out of MY Mouth. 17Because thou sayest, I am rich, and increased with goods, and have need of nothing; and knowest not that thou art wretched, and miserable, and poor, and blind, and naked:

Acts 19

Words of the LORD:

"Don't Be Found Outside Of MY Will Or I Will Reject And Cast You Away."

(Words Received from Our LORD by Susan, January 22, 2013)

MY children, your LORD Speaketh:

I am coming. Make no mistake, I have promised and what GOD Says, HE Does. Few believe ME—few truly are moved by these Words and encouragement. I know because I see ALL—I know ALL and I see who pursues ME, follows ME, loves ME above ALL else and all others.

There is no shortage of those who pursue the world, who seek answers through those who deny I exist and reject MY Truth. Soon Truth will be hard to come by. Already it is a diminishing commodity. MY Truth is Priceless Gold—its value cannot be measured as MY Truth leads to MY Kingdom of Eternal Life with ALMIGHTY GOD—CREATOR of the Universe. The value of this Truth cannot be measured or calculated. Few seek it although it is available—readily found. Only those ardent for Truth seek it with all their hearts, souls, minds, and strength—those who surrender their ALL and cling to their GOD. These find Truth—a wellspring of peace, wholeness, and eternal salvation.

MY Priceless Truth cannot be replaced or discovered through many paths though many believe it so. There is only ONE TRUE PATH to the ULTIMATE TRUTH: I AM THE WAY—THE NARROW ROAD. FULL surrender to ME: LORD WHO was crucified for the transgressions of all men through acts of sin treason against the Ways of a Holy, Just GOD. I laid MY Life down, gave ALL, endured torture for sin-filled mankind. I was bruised, scourged, spat upon, beaten, and I became the punishment for all men. This was the price MY FATHER would accept for the sins of all men for whosoever would lay their life down, submit themselves over to ME and choose ME as LORD and MASTER.

There is no other way—only MY WAY—MY Gift, MY Price Paid. Although there appears to be many ways, there is only ONE WAY, through ME and the Baptism of the HOLY SPIRIT.

The world is falling apart. All seems well. This is because you refuse to look to see. You must see the hour you live in—time is running out. You must see the times you are living in and to see this you must read MY Book and receive eye salve from MY SPIRIT to receive understanding of the Words you are reading. Only HE can open your eyes to the meaning of the Words in MY Holy Book. This is essential to being ready for what is coming: the rescue of MY ready bride and tribulation meant for those who choose against ME and are left behind.

Face ME, surrender your ALL. Find safe keeping in the Perfect Will of GOD. Don't be found outside of MY Will or I will reject and cast you away.

Come now. Live in peace with your GOD.

I Love you,

LORD YAHUSHUA

Coordinating Scripture

Numbers 23:19:, GOD is not a man, that HE should lie; neither the son of man, that HE should repent: hath HE said, and shall HE not do it? Or hath HE spoken, and shall HE not make it good?

Psalm 85:10, Mercy and truth are met together; righteousness and peace have kissed each other.

1 Corinthians 6:20, For ye are bought with a price: therefore glorify GOD in your body, and in your spirit, which are GOD's.

Matthew 7:21, Not everyone that saith unto ME, LORD, LORD, shall enter into the kingdom of heaven; but he that doeth the Will of MY FATHER which is in heaven.

CHAPTER 3

They Are On A Landslide Down A Mountain And They Don't Even Know It

Wed, 6 Feb 2013

The LORD's Words:

"They Are On A Landslide Down A Mountain And They Don't Even Know It."

We have all been deceived. We cling to our TVs, movies, hobbies, and worldly pursuits like they are gold. We have filled our days with the "inferior" and have only left tiny openings of our lives to the "superior." We've had the wool pulled over our eyes big time.

We think the things of this world are so wonderful, futuristic, "ahead of its time" and at the same time we have classified GOD as a "has been" old guy who looks like someone's Great Grandpa. In reality, we live in a cursed, dying, and decaying world but not GOD.

We've been royally fooled by the master deceiver. We pursue the technology and creations of men as if men are gods over their own destiny. We have been duped. We look at the buildings, inventions, and creations of men and worship these things like they are unparalleled.

We are trading the pursuit of the works of our own CREATOR for that of the creation. We marvel at robots and forget that GOD created humans...we go crazy over the latest aircraft and forget GOD Created all the winged living breathing creatures in their incredible complexity. We absorb all our time reading the writings of humans and make no time for the Book that is GOD-Breathed and

23

Inspired—the Bible. We fill our days listening to every humanistic view on the TV, radio, and Internet—and we never make time to commune and talk to our own CREATOR—although HE Calls us to HIMSELF and makes it known that HE listens, cares, and amazingly desires our company.

We say there is no time for GOD—what a shame…

We MUST make time for GOD—HE Created us for HIS Pleasure. If you don't figure this out really quickly—you are going to find yourself outside of the access to your own CREATOR, MAKER for ALL eternity.

This is radical: STOP being deceived! Turn off your TVs. Stop wasting time on going to movies. Quit throwing yourself into your hobbies and worldly pursuits. Instead, give your life to GOD…give HIM your most precious commodities: your soul and your time. Spend your time getting to know GOD: talk to HIM (prayer) and read HIS Book (the Bible). You won't regret it. You will regret not doing this—I guarantee it.

Below the LORD's Letters are NEW visions from readers. At the very bottom of this letter is a list of the past letters from the LORD covering many important topics relevant to the times we are living in.

Also below is an invitation to download and read the FREE MARRIAGE SUPPER OF THE LAMB Ebook with Words from the LORD for this end time generation. THIS BOOK IS CHANGING LIVES! ANNOUNCING IN THIS LETTER: Thanks to Alejandro Zurita there are now audios of the MARRIAGE SUPPER OF THE LAMB book in SPANISH—see below! Plus sign up to receive the hottest ever end times headlines coming across our desks in the

End Times News Report we put out each week. Plus the latest words/visions from young brothers Jonathan and Sebastian and Buddy Baker. Also, to read past letters from the LORD you can visit this link:

http://end-times-prophecy.com/blog/?category_name=2012-the-lords-messages

ANNOUNCING IN THIS LETTER: FREE DOWNLOAD OF THE BOOK IN LOVE WITH THE WHIRLWIND by Susan Davis (with thanks to Mike Peralta for preparing the Ebook). Interview about IN LOVE WITH THE WHIRLWIND:

http://sites.radiantwebtools.com/index.cfm?i=11265&mid=12&id=18641

Free Ebook download for IN LOVE WITH THE WHIRLWIND:

https://www.smashwords.com/books/view/280038

Special Note: New links for Deborah Melissa Moller's book, "The Final Call" now also in Spanish—see below with the Final Call information.

Words of the LORD:

"They Are On A Landslide Down A Mountain And They Don't Even Know It."

(Words Received from Our LORD by Susan, January 29-30, 2013— Just a side note about this letter: when the LORD gave me the words about a "landslide" I was taken back that this was a really different Word from the LORD. The next day I was stunned to learn that Indonesia had experienced two different landslide disasters the days before that I knew nothing about—I was just amazed by this. Here is the report I received after I took down this amazing word: http://www.abc.net.au/news/2013-01-29/deadly-sumatra-landslide-wipes-out-homes/4488052)

Let US begin:

There is a rude awakening coming to this world. Many are not paying attention. They cannot see the writing on the wall. They do not read MY Book. They are far from ME in their ways. They are on a landslide down a mountain and they don't even know it. The world is cascading downward and the people are fixed in their lukewarm churches fondling the things of the world like dogs in heat.

Church of the lukewarm: you are lukewarm if you don't make ME first in your life and surrender your ALL to ME. It doesn't matter how many times you sit in your churches. I don't care about your buildings—I want your heart, mind, soul, and spirit. I want to know that you are ONE with ME—your LORD and MAKER.

I Created you.

I Breathed life in you.

I filled you with life's breath.

Now you live and have your being. You are an eternal being, just where will you spend eternity?

Will it be with your GOD ETERNAL or with MY enemy in hell fire and torment?

Think these hard Words? Hard words are words of deception MY enemy puts out telling you all is right between us when you are sleeping around with the world and rejecting your GOD.

MY church has grown fond of the pleasant Words they take from MY Truth and then they leave out the other Words—Words that would change their lives if they would read them. These Words include: "Love your neighbor as yourself,"…"Seek after the LORD with all your heart, mind, soul, strength,"…"Do unto others as you would have them do unto you." These are all precepts to follow that would change the hearts of every man, woman, and child if MY people would listen and follow them.

I am not a GOD WHO makes things hard and oppressive. MY Yoke is light. MY enemy is the one who makes the people carry a heavy burden. He is the one to which hardships of mankind can be attributed.

Men struggle because they do not really pursue ME. If they did they would find their perfect place in life—the one I set out for their life when I Created them and their lives would go as they were meant to go. Apart from the ONE True Narrow Path laid out for every human to follow for their own life, people will follow all sorts of evil courses that the enemy tempts them to take. They end up falling into ditches of deception. Many believe they are on the right course and they will be shocked to find themselves outside MY Specific Will for their life and sadly most will fall into hell. This is the course of most human beings because they refuse to follow ME, their GOD.

Come back to ME before it is too late. You can change the course you are on at any moment and come to the right path for your life and to peace with your GOD. You just need to lay down your life before ME, surrender your ALL—give ME a FULL SURRENDER from the depths of your spirit: a strong desire to be right with GOD, pursuing GOD's Perfect Plan for your life. Those who hunger and thirst after righteousness will be filled. Come be filled with MY OIL for your lamp.

There has never been a better time to get right with your GOD. MY enemy is about to take over the world and I am coming to save MY people, MY true church from death and destruction. Waken to this Truth. Time is closing down.

This is the GOD of your fathers

HOLY WONDER from Above,

MIGHTY FORTRESS,

PRINCE of PEACE,

I AM the ALPHA and OMEGA,

ETERNAL LIGHT.

Come, Let ME Consume you.

Coordinating Scripture:

Proverbs 26:11, As a dog returneth to his vomit, so a fool returneth to his folly.

2 Peter 2:20-22, 20For if after they have escaped the pollutions of the world through the knowledge of the LORD and SAVIOUR JESUS CHRIST, they are again entangled therein, and overcome, the latter end is worse with them than the beginning. 21For it had been better for them not to have known the way of righteousness,

than, after they have known it, to turn from the holy commandment delivered unto them. 22But it is happened unto them according to the true proverb, The dog is turned to his own vomit again; and the sow that was washed to her wallowing in the mire.

Acts 17:27, That they should seek the LORD, if haply they might feel after HIM, and find HIM, though he be not far from every one of us:

Matthew 22:36-40, 36MASTER, which is the great commandment in the law? 37JESUS said unto him, Thou shalt love the LORD thy GOD with all thy heart, and with all thy soul, and with all thy mind. 38This is the first and great commandment. 39And the second is like unto it, Thou shalt love thy neighbour as thyself. 40On these two commandments hang all the law and the prophets.

Luke 6:31, And as ye would that men should do to you, do ye also to them likewise.

Matthew 11:29, Take MY Yoke upon you, and learn of ME; for I am meek and lowly in heart: and ye shall find rest unto your souls.

Words of the LORD:

"I Will Love Them Like A Man Loves His Only Son…"

(Words Received from Our LORD by Susan, January 31, 2013)

I (GOD) can give you Words:

MY children, I am your FATHER. I am the ONE you can count on when things look dark and trouble grows. I want you to know that there is nothing too big for your GOD. I am ALL-encompassing. I am a FORCE to be reckoned with. Nothing gets by ME.

I know all from beginning to end of each person's life. Although men give ME no heed in their lives that does not mean I do not exist, regardless of what men think or believe about ME. I am alive and in charge over humanity and the Universe. If anything at all happens, it is because I allow it.

MY enemy rules by intimidation and fear. He controls by deception, lies, and half truths. MY children believe in the lies of the enemy and fall prey to his schemes. If only they would turn to ME: surrender their ALL to ME, then they would be free of the control of MY enemy. Very few find this freedom. Very few are set free from the invisible chains that bind them by the power of MY rival.

The people believe his lies and fall into a whole range of troubles. MY enemy will try any and all tricks to capture MY children. He knows their weaknesses.

Come into MY Light—Light is where Truth is. When you are in the dark, you won't know what you need to save yourself from the deception of a cruel enemy. This is how to be safe: surrender to ME fully: you must desire it more than anything else. It is not about your head knowledge: it is about the passion of your heart.

MY church is passionate for ME. She seeks ME all through the day. She knows I am the SOURCE of all love, comfort, strength—no other loves so completely. You can look nowhere else to have your needs met. Stop looking for answers and solutions in places these cannot be found. Turn to ME, your ONE True SOURCE of Life Eternal.

MY people know I am coming soon. They are watching, waiting, and warning others. These will come with ME into Glory. I am holding a beautiful place for each one of them: MY choicest treasures. I will love them like a man loves his only son.

Come be part of this Great Mystery unfolding: the life to come for the bride of CHRIST in her eternal home.

Make your way to ME before the door closes completely.

I AM the SACRIFICIAL LAMB WHO taketh away the sins of the world...

Coordinating Scripture:

Jeremiah 32:27, Behold, I am the LORD, the GOD of all flesh: is there anything too hard for ME?

Revelation 12:9, And the great dragon was cast out, that old serpent, called the devil, and satan, which deceiveth the whole world:

Exodus 32:14, And the LORD repented of the evil which HE thought to do unto HIS people.

Romans 6:23, For the wages of sin is death; but the gift of GOD is eternal life through JESUS CHRIST our LORD.

1 Corinthians 15:51-52, Behold, I shew you a mystery; We shall not all sleep, but we shall all be changed, 52In a moment, in the twinkling of an eye, at the last trump: for the trumpet shall sound, and the dead shall be raised incorruptible, and we shall be changed.

CHAPTER 4

Only Those Who Are In MY Will, Will Come With ME

Sun, 17 Feb 2013

The LORD's Words:

"Only Those Who Are In MY Will, Will Come With ME"

MY TESTIMONY.

The LORD was doing miraculous things in my life and I had several friends wanting me to write a book about it all, but I hated the idea of writing a book. Then the LORD put it on my heart to do it because I believed that I could share my faith and experiences with many of my lost friends and family through a book format. It took me a long time to create a book manuscript, but after I did, I went to the LORD and said, "Well I have the manuscript done and if YOU want me to do a book, YOU are going to have to send me the money for it because I can't do this for free." Exactly two days later, the money came to me in a miraculous way and I could no longer deny that this was what GOD wanted for me to do. The book is called: IN LOVE WITH THE WHIRLWIND. Here is a link to more info on the book: http://sites.radiantwebtools.com/index.cfm?i=11265&mid=12&id=18 641 and here is a Free Ebook download for IN LOVE WITH THE WHIRLWIND: https://www.smashwords.com/books/view/280038

THIS UNIQUE MINISTRY

Before the book was completed, I was working hard for a secular company. The LORD sent someone to me to tell me the LORD wanted me to work for HIM. I did not believe this and then a few months later, I was forced to leave my company because of an "ethics" issue. It was then the LORD revealed to me a second time that HE wanted me to work for HIM exclusively. I told HIM that I would do it, but that I had to have some kind of financial support in order to work full time for HIM—once again, exactly two days later, out of the blue, a call came and I received financial support which came completely unexpectedly enabling me to do exactly what the LORD wanted me to do: work full time for HIM.

About this time, I received the amazing gift of being able to hear the LORD's Voice and I began to receive these End Time Letters from the LORD that HE wanted to be sent out. Incredibly, the HOLY SPIRIT continues to send people to do their parts in this ministry: our publisher, the web people, translators, pastoral support, and volunteers for various projects. It has been overwhelming to see the LORD work things out. It was not too long ago that I received the incredible Word from the LORD HIMSELF that this ministry I am involved in is specifically for the preparation of the bride of CHRIST for the coming rapture. If you have been compelled to read the messages put out by the LORD through this ministry it is because the HOLY SPIRIT has drawn you and is preparing you to be the bride of CHRIST. This is a true Word.

WORDS FOR THE BRIDE

One day a year ago, the LORD called me to do a forty day fast at our family cabin away from my family. I knew the LORD was dealing with me over some personal issues but I had no idea that from it would become the book: MARRIAGE SUPPER OF THE LAMB. The book is a complete series of Letters from the LORD about the end times and the LORD's soon return. While I was struggling through my forty day fast, the LORD gave me a letter daily and sometimes two letters. There is not one letter in the book that required rewrites, additions, deletions, or changes—all are pure Words from the

33

Throne of GOD. After I came back with the document, I sent it to my publisher who immediately produced it into book form and now it is available to anyone who wants to download it free:

https://www.smashwords.com/books/view/162979

TWO NEW BOOKS SOON-TO-BE-RELEASED FOR THE BRIDE

Now I am pleased to announce that we will soon be releasing as free downloadable books the collection of Letters from the LORD since last March 2012 with end time warnings for the soon approaching return of CHRIST. The books are titled: RAPTURE OR TRIBULATION and LEFT BEHIND AFTER THE RAPTURE. These books will be free downloadable books available to you and to send to your friends.

Thank you for your support and kind words. God bless you, Susan

Jeremiah 1:17, Thou therefore gird up thy loins, and arise, and speak unto them all that I command thee: be not dismayed at their faces, lest I confound thee before them.

Words of the LORD:

"The Holiness Of MY World To Come For MY Bride Will Take Your Breath Away."

(Words Received from Our LORD by Susan, February 8, 2013)

MY daughter, I can give you Words:

Children, it is your LORD—HIGH and MIGHTY!

I am Coming for MY church. She is making herself ready. She is beautiful in MY Sight. I long to take her home to show her white, pristine holiness of the Kingdom to come. She has not experienced the holiness that awaits her in this life. The holiness of MY World to come for MY bride will take your breath away.

Everyone in MY Kingdom have robes of purity, unmarred, perfect in every way—perfected by the Power of MY HOLY SPIRIT. There is strength and power that flows through MY Heavenly Kingdom. Everyone is fully submitted to the Power of MY SPIRIT and the atmosphere is electrical: energized with Power from MY Great Throne. This Power will seize a man, take him over, cause him to live pure and perfect in MY Sight. There is pleasure with this Power—the pleasure that comes from MY Right Hand...the reward that is due all MY saints who submit their lives to ME willingly in this life: who seek ME in all their ways; who chase after ME in their hearts; lay down the love for this world and its evil in exchange for a desire to live righteously before GOD.

Rewards increase daily in this life to those who choose to come into MY Will—who want to be aligned with MY Heart; MY Views; MY Thoughts. Those who have a servant's heart toward those around them will discover the treasures of MY Heart: everlasting pleasure in the Kingdom of GOD.

Don't let the short-lived temptations of this life and the flesh fool you. Yes, sin is pleasurable for a time, but soon it turns to death and destruction to those who refuse to seek GOD and choose to be free of the sin pulling them down. Turn to follow ME and I will show you a new way of life. Lay your burdens at MY Feet and let ME begin to turn your cold heart back to a warm heart of flesh. You cannot do this apart from MY HOLY SPIRIT Power. It is impossible in your own human power—try though you may to conquer sin, apart from

ME and MY Blood Covering you will fall short every time and fall back into sin's clutches.

Don't let sin and MY enemy rule over you. Flee from him and run to ME. Soon it will be too late to walk through MY open door to safety that is now available to MY bride. Once I bring her out at MY side away from this troubled world the door will shut and those left will have to contend with MY enemy. Many will die in their sins, cast into hell for eternity. Many will face hard times at the hands of evil men controlled by demons. This will be the fate of those who turn to ME after the bride is removed.

Come with ME NOW. Choose for ME NOW. Relinquish the control of the world and follow your SAVIOR. Only you can make this choice. Many will fall away out of stubbornness of heart. You can avoid this end. There is NO other way.

Come away with ME. I can save you. It is MY Desire.

Your LORD and SAVIOR

YAHUSHUA

Coordinating Scripture:

Ephesians 5:25-27, 25Husbands, love your wives, even as CHRIST also loved the church, and gave HIMSELF for it; 26That HE might sanctify and cleanse it with the washing of water by the word, 27That HE might present it to HIMSELF a glorious church, not having spot, or wrinkle, or any such thing; but that it should be holy and without blemish.

1 Corinthians 4:20, For the kingdom of GOD is not in word, but in power.

Psalm 16:11, THOU wilt shew me the path of life: in THY presence is fullness of joy; at THY Right Hand there are pleasures for evermore.

James 1:14-15, 14But every man is tempted, when he is drawn away of his own lust, and enticed. 15Then when lust hath conceived, it bringeth forth sin: and sin, when it is finished, bringeth forth death.

Ezekiel 36:26, A new heart also will I give you, and a new spirit will I put within you: and I will take away the stony heart out of your flesh, and I will give you an heart of flesh.

Words of the LORD:

"Only Those Who Are In MY Will, Will Come With ME When I Remove MY Church To Safety."

(Words Received from Our LORD by Susan, February 9, 2013)

Let US begin:

Children, let ME show you something new. I am a Great and Powerful GOD. I am able to change even the hardest hearts and change those who love ME the least. Stand in the gap for those you love—bend your knee for them. Pray earnestly. Remember, I am looking for those who will come to the aid of their brothers, sisters, neighbors, fathers, mothers, and lost children.

Pray from a heart desperate to see those around you saved from eternal hell. It is MY Promise to answer the prayers of those who truly seek MY Will: surrender your ALL to ME, lay your life down at MY Feet—even your own future plans. Then, I can hear your prayers for your lost family and friends—heal their cold hearts and lead them back to their GOD, but you must first do your part. Submit yourself to MY Will, allow ME to use your life to save others around you.

You must desire to die to your own plans to allow ME to use your life as I see fit—then and only then, will your prayers have true Power. Is it not worth it to save others? Ultimately you will also save yourself. Only those who are in MY Will, will come with ME when I remove MY church to safety. If you are outside MY Will and not fully surrendered to ME, I will shut the door and you will be standing outside, left behind to a cruel outcome: great tribulation, torment, torture.

So come, kneel, surrender your will, submit to your GOD. Receive MY Blood Ransom and Covering. Receive MY Love and Eternal Life. Come claim your eternal inheritance I have for you in MY Heavenlies. This is waiting for you: salvation for you and your loved ones. Press into the prize set before you. The hour is truly late.

Love your LORD and SAVIOR

Romans 9:18, Therefore hath HE mercy on whom HE will have mercy, and whom HE will HE hardeneth.

Daniel 10:12, Then said he unto me, Fear not, Daniel: for from the first day that thou didst set thine heart to understand, and to chasten thyself before thy GOD, thy words were heard, and I am come for thy words.

Proverbs 15:29, The LORD is far from the wicked: but HE heareth the prayer of the righteous.

1 Peter 3:12, For the Eyes of the LORD are over the righteous, and HIS Ears are open unto their prayers: but the Face of the LORD is against them that do evil.

Matthew 25:10, And while they went to buy, the bridegroom came; and they that were ready went in with him to the marriage: and the door was shut.

1 Peter 1:3-4, 3Blessed be the GOD and FATHER of our LORD JESUS CHRIST, which according to HIS abundant mercy hath begotten us again unto a lively hope by the resurrection of JESUS CHRIST from the dead, 4To an inheritance incorruptible, and undefiled, and that fadeth not away, reserved in heaven for you

CHAPTER 5

Come Out Of The World And Her Lies

Fri, 1 Mar 2013

The LORD's Words:

"Come Out Of The World, Come Apart From Her Lies: The Traditions Of Men And Hatred For The Move Of MY SPIRIT"

Who should be talking about the concept of being holy? EVERYONE should be talking about the importance of pursuing holiness. We ALL should be talking about it. If college and high school basketball players had never talked about aspiring to go "PRO" there would have never been any NBA players.

So just exactly what does GOD's Word have to say about us being "holy?" 1 Peter 1:16 says: Because it is written, Be ye holy; for I am holy. And, Ephesians 5:27 says: That HE might present it to HIMSELF a glorious church, not having spot, or wrinkle, or any such thing; but that it should be holy and without blemish.

Then the bible goes on to say this: 1 Peter 4:18, And if the righteous scarcely be saved, where shall the ungodly and the sinner appear? And this in Matthew 7:14 says: Because strait is the gate, and narrow is the way, which leadeth unto life, and FEW there be that find it.

WOW—holiness is REQUIRED to enter heaven and FEW are acquiring this holiness, according to the Scripture. This alone should cause more people to want to talk about holiness and understand it…

So just how "Holy" is GOD anyway? Well Scripture says this in Job 15:15, Behold, HE putteth no trust in HIS saints; yea, the Heavens are not clean in HIS Sight. WOW again: GOD puts no trust in HIS people and even the Heavens are not pure enough for HIM.

GOD says this in Romans 3:10-12, 10As it is written, There is none righteous, no, not one: 11There is none that understandeth, there is none that seeketh after GOD. 12They are all gone out of the way, they are together become unprofitable; there is none that doeth good, no, not one. Also in Job 14:4 it says: Who can bring a clean thing out of an unclean? Not one.

So we, apart from GOD's involvement, cannot clean up our acts or even want to pursue GOD. But according to Mark 10:27 it says: And JESUS looking upon them saith: With men it is impossible, but not with GOD: for with GOD ALL things are possible.

Although we have nothing going for us—with GOD we can do what seems impossible: pursue holiness. Matthew 5:6 says: Blessed are they which do hunger and thirst after righteousness: for they shall be FILLED. Having a sincere hunger and thirst for righteousness will bring you a FILLING of the HOLY SPIRIT: the same kind of HOLY SPIRIT FILLING mentioned in the parable of the 10 virgins in Matthew 25:1-4, Then shall the Kingdom of Heaven be likened unto ten virgins, which took their lamps, and went forth to meet the bridegroom. 2And five of them were wise, and five were foolish. 3They that were foolish took their lamps, and took no oil with them: 4But the wise took oil in their vessels with their lamps.

The definition of "Holy" is to be set apart from evil. So if you are set apart from evil or "Holy" you are FILLED with the HOLY SPIRIT Who leads you away from evil. Galatians 3:6 says: Even as Abraham believed GOD, and it was accounted to him for righteousness. So, Abraham was righteous because he believed GOD. Abraham would have lived by the verse Matthew 22:37, 37JESUS said unto him, Thou shalt love the LORD THY GOD with all thy heart, and with all thy soul, and with all thy mind.

Abraham FILLED himself with GOD—and his focus would have been on GOD. And because of this, GOD called Abraham "Righteous" or "Holy" because he was FILLED with a belief in GOD. And because of his consuming belief in GOD there was no room for the things of the world.

Today, anyone who wants to be FILLED with the HOLY SPIRIT and believes in GOD can ask for it and receive it. There is nothing that is keeping you from this except your desire. Doubt leads to disobedience and disobedience leads to disaster.

Preparing for the LORD's Return:

1. Repent, forgive all, BELIEVE that the LORD died for your sins and confess your faith to others.

2. Surrender your ALL to the LORD (future plans also).

3. Pray to be covered by the Blood of CHRIST

4. Ask to have a FULL oil lamp and to be FILLED with the HOLY SPIRIT

5. Read your Bible daily

Words of the LORD:

"Too Many Would Rather Sit In Front Of And Worship Dead, Lifeless Idols Than Seek The Face Of The Living GOD"

(Words Received from Our LORD by Susan, February 20, 2013)

This Letter is for whoever will listen:

I am GOD. I reign from Above. MY Countenance is of Pure Light. MY Presence is everywhere although you don't see ME; MY Presence can be felt and experienced by those who seek MY Face with all their heart, soul, mind, strength.

It is MY Desire to be sought out by MY people. Very few come looking. Choices must be made. Too many are caught up in the ways of the world. Too many would rather sit in front of and worship dead, lifeless idols than seek the Face of the Living GOD, the CREATOR of all life, the MAKER of their soul. This is a sad state of affairs. At the end of it all, when you stand before ME as all MY children will, I will say, "I never knew you—depart from ME, ye workers of iniquity." You will then leave to your eternal destination which is hell everlasting.

This will happen. Most men are assigned to hell because their hands desired the dead idols and sins of their flesh over the Living, Life Giving, Breathing GOD of all. This was their choice to make and choices have consequences. So you are at a critical juncture. You can choose for ME, your GOD or against ME for MY enemy. There is no middle ground.

Your lack of a choice for ME is still a choice against ME. Thou lukewarm: I will spit you out. Your half-hearted love for ME brings ME no pleasure. Half of your heart belongs to your own worldly passions and ultimately to MY enemy. You are all his unless you are all MINE. Do you not understand this, MY children?

Read MY Word. Get to know MY Plan for your life—MY Ways are higher and loftier than yours. I have Great Plans for your life now and for eternity in MY Beautiful Kingdom. There is love and passion waiting for you: a love you will never find in your empty, worldly pursuits that you cling to so desperately.

Submit to ME fully, surrender your ALL. Make ME LORD, MASTER, SAVIOR, ALL IN ALL. I want it ALL. Second best will not do. You either desire MY Company in this world as your ALL IN ALL or you do not belong to ME. This is MY Way, although few find it, very few. The Way is Narrow, but for those who find it, a banquet of delight awaits.

Surrender your ALL. Repent of your sins. You cannot make yourself clean enough for a Holy GOD apart from ME and MY Power, so surrender as you are and leave the rest to ME: the AUTHOR and FINISHER of your faith. Come experience the love you were made to receive. I am waiting and then I will come to take out MY bride. The hour has now become shorter.

Don't put your very soul at risk. Your loss will be great.

I am the LOVER of your soul,

Yahushua ha Mashiach

Coordinating Scripture:

Isaiah 44:14-17, 14 He heweth him down cedars, and taketh the cypress and the oak, which he strengtheneth for himself among the trees of the forest: he planteth an ash, and the rain doth nourish it. 15 Then shall it be for a man to burn: for he will take thereof, and warm himself; yea, he kindleth it, and baketh bread; yea, he maketh a god, and worshippeth it; he maketh it a graven image, and falleth down thereto. 16 He burneth part thereof in the fire; with part thereof he eateth flesh; he roasteth roast, and is satisfied: yea, he warmeth himself, and saith, Aha, I am warm, I have seen the fire: 17 And the residue thereof he maketh a god, even his graven image: he falleth down unto it, and worshippeth it, and prayeth unto it, and saith, Deliver me; for thou art my god.

Hebrews 12:2, Looking unto JESUS the AUTHOR and FINISHER of our faith; WHO for the joy that was set before HIM endured the cross, despising the shame, and is set down at the right hand of the throne of GOD.

Matthew 7:14, Because strait is the gate, and narrow is the way, which leadeth unto life, and few there be that find it.

Words of the LORD:

"Come Out Of The World, Come Apart From Her Lies: The Traditions Of Men And Hatred For The Move Of MY SPIRIT"

(Words Received from Our LORD by Susan, February 21, 2013)

Write MY Words:

Children, I your LORD come to you in distress—I am facing the near removal of MY church out of the clutches of evil but in exchange for that action, the world remaining will see destruction and ongoing woes.

Mankind has chosen against ME, its GOD, MAKER. The hour is arriving to save the few who have really chosen for ME against the pull of the world and the lust of their own ways. This number is few although MY messengers continue to reveal this Truth and MY Book speaks plainly of this. You continue to disregard this warning as if it does not apply to you and those around you—as if you have special immunity to MY Words and Truth.

MY flock leaders also believe lies and try to tell themselves another interpretation of MY Word. The churches believe they will see a great many saved before the last hour of MY Return for MY bride. They are sorely mistaken, puffed up, stiff necked, full of the words they, themselves, most want to hear: the words that tickle their ears. They do not move in MY SPIRIT and they are not hearing MY Truth. I am not a man that I should lie.

Very few will be released from the evil coming over the earth, once the RESTRAINER is taken out of the way—MY SPIRIT. Few will avoid the hardship of Great Tribulation. This should make you tremble, bring you to your knees, cause you to be dissatisfied with the lies and deception of the world leading you astray.

Come out of the world, come apart from her lies: the traditions of men and hatred for the move of MY SPIRIT and all of HIS HOLY Manifestations in your churches—white wash tombs. Do you not know that MY SPIRIT and I are ONE? Can you not understand this? When you reject the supernatural power of MY SPIRIT because it is too much for you—you reject your SAVIOR, the ONE WHO paid your ransom on the cross of pain and suffering.

Soon, I am coming for those who love ME—ALL of ME: MY SPIRIT, MY TRUTH, MY WAYS, MY POWER. Those whose scales have come off their eyes will see ME when I come. The rest who still have scales over their eyes will miss MY Coming, but they will know I came and went without them. O' what sadness will come over those who follow ME in their minds but not in their hearts. O' the loss when they see what their cold hearts will have to face at the hands of MY enemy. Then their cold hearts will melt finally, in despair, and they will have to drink the cup of bitterness to come into MY Kingdom. This is coming—even at the door.

So gird yourself, put on your armor, surrender your ALL, and repent for trying to conquer sin in your own power because you reject the move of MY SPIRIT in your life. Read MY Word, get familiar with Truth. You are running out of time…

THE ALPHA AND OMEGA HAS SPOKEN

Coordinating Scripture:

Ephesians 4:30, And grieve not the HOLY SPIRIT of GOD, whereby ye are sealed unto the day of redemption.

Luke 17:26-30, 26And as it was in the days of Noah, so shall it be also in the days of the SON of man. 27They did eat, they drank, they married wives, they were given in marriage, until the day that Noah entered into the ark, and the flood came, and destroyed them all. 28Likewise also as it was in the days of Lot; they did eat, they drank, they bought, they sold, they planted, they builded; 29But the same day that Lot went out of Sodom it rained fire and brimstone from heaven, and destroyed them all. 30Even thus shall it be in the day when the SON of man is revealed.

Jeremiah 17:23, But they obeyed not, neither inclined their ear, but made their neck stiff, that they might not hear, nor receive instruction.

2 Timothy 4:3, For the time will come when they will not endure sound doctrine; but after their own lusts shall they heap to themselves teachers, having itching ears;

2 Thessalonians 2:7, For the mystery of iniquity doth already work: only HE WHO now letteth will let, until he be taken out of the way.

Matthew 23:27-28, 27Woe unto you, scribes and Pharisees, hypocrites! for ye are like unto whited sepulchres, which indeed appear beautiful outward, but are within full of dead men's bones, and of all uncleanness. 28Even so ye also outwardly appear righteous unto men, but within ye are full of hypocrisy and iniquity.

Romans 7:4-5, 4Wherefore, my brethren, ye also are become dead to the law by the Body of CHRIST; that ye should be married to another, even to HIM WHO is raised from the dead, that we should bring forth fruit unto GOD. 5For when we were in the flesh, the motions of sins, which were by the law, did work in our members to bring forth fruit unto death.

CHAPTER 6

Those Who Follow ME Closely Will Escape The Evil

Thu, 7 Mar 2013

The LORD's Words:

"Those Who Follow ME Closely Will Escape The Evil Coming To Destroy The People Left Behind."

Many, even Christians, don't believe in the event called the rapture. "Rapture" is the event the bible speaks of in which the true followers of CHRIST (also known as the bride of CHRIST) will be supernaturally removed prior to the advent of tribulation or Great Tribulation, (that was forewarned in the bible) comes on the world.

Now, many do not believe in the rapture event and say the Christians are doomed for tribulation. Well that is partially true—the "lukewarm" Christians (the same who the LORD says HE will spit them out) will be left behind to face tribulation or sudden destruction. The lukewarm are those who are partially interested in the LORD and yet also very much interested in participating in worldly activities and still embracing the world—GOD says the world is an enmity to HIM and you cannot serve BOTH: GOD and mammon. Matthew 6:24, No man can serve two masters: for either he will hate the one, and love the other; or else he will hold to the one, and despise the other. Ye cannot serve GOD and mammon.

There is a group of Christians who say there is no rapture event at all and we are all doomed to suffer tribulation. This group is partially right. They, themselves will not be raptured. Their lack of belief in the rapture and subsequent promotion of the "no rapture" concept to

49

others will guarantee that they indeed will not be experiencing the rapture themselves when it occurs.

The Bible says this: 2 Timothy 4:8, Henceforth there is laid up for me a crown of righteousness, which the LORD, the RIGHTEOUS JUDGE, shall give me at that day: and not to me only, but unto all them also that love HIS Appearing. This particular scripture describes people who are rewarded with a Crown of Righteousness from the LORD for longing for HIS Return. To receive the Crown of Righteousness, you need to be "looking" for a RESCUING GOD and not a god who is sending his devoted people (bride) into hopelessness and tribulation—two completely different looks here.

The Bible says this: Matthew 24:42-44, 42Watch therefore: for ye know not what hour your LORD doth come. 43But know this, that if the goodman of the house had known in what watch the thief would come, he would have watched, and would not have suffered his house to be broken up. 44Therefore be ye also ready: for in such an hour as ye think not the SON of man cometh. Once again the LORD is coming like a thief according to this passage of scripture. The people are told "to be ready." This scripture describes people who are ready, waiting and told to watch, therefore: this would not describe a group of hopeless, dejected Christians assigned to suffer through Great Tribulation—again, two completely different looks.

Those who are NOT watching for the rapture—won't be going because only watchers, who are looking for the LORD's Return, are turning away from the hopelessness of the world to come toward a bright future with the LORD. In fact, by denying that the rapture event is true those who say there is no rapture in the Bible are speaking death into their situation and not a blessing and they are delivering themselves into tribulation by the power of their own words or cursings over themselves: Deuteronomy 30:19, I call heaven and earth to record this day against you, that I have set before you life and death, blessing and cursing: therefore choose life, that both thou and thy seed may live. Many people say the word rapture is not in the bible and they want to write off the rapture event altogether. Oh really? The rapture event actually has many scripture references, including these verses:

1 Thessalonians 4:17, Then we which are alive and remain shall be caught up together with them in the clouds, to meet the LORD in the air: and so shall we ever be with the LORD.

1 Corinthians 15:52, In a moment, in the twinkling of an eye, at the last trump: for the trumpet shall sound, and the dead shall be raised incorruptible, and we shall be changed.

Mark 13:32-37, 32But of that day and that hour knoweth no man, no, not the angels which are in heaven, neither the SON, but the FATHER. 33Take ye heed, watch and pray: for ye know not when the time is. 34For the SON of Man is as a man taking a far journey, who left his house, and gave authority to his servants, and to every man his work, and commanded the porter to watch. 35Watch ye therefore: for ye know not when the master of the house cometh, at even, or at midnight, or at the cockcrowing, or in the morning: 36Lest coming suddenly he find you sleeping. 37And what I say unto you I say unto all, Watch.

Here are additional "rapture" verses describing the upcoming, undeniable rapture event:

http://www.bibleprophesy.org/rapture.htm#more

http://www.openbible.info/topics/the_rapture

http://www.pretribulation.com/passages2.htm

Words of the LORD:

"Those Who Follow ME Closely Will Escape The Evil Coming To Destroy The People Left Behind."

(Words Received from Our LORD by Susan, March 4, 2013)

I am ready for you to write MY Words:

Soon MY children your LORD will appear in the sky. I will remove MY church. I will take you home with ME. We will fly to the heights. Those who follow ME closely will escape the evil coming to destroy the people left behind. There is a wave of destruction moving across the land—it is the result of evil.

Evil is the movement away from a Holy GOD to choose for rebellion against your GOD, your MAKER. It is an affront against MY Will to reject MY Ways, MY Truth, MY Light. It is a movement to embrace darkness and the ways of MY enemy, who is bent on destroying all that I, GOD, hold dear.

I am allowing this darkness. I cannot reward rebellion, disobedience, and willful evil against MY Ways and Truth. The things of the world you see coming about should come as no surprise to you if you read MY Word. You know that the wages of sin is death and now there is a wave of death moving across the world as a direct result of blatant sin against MY Holy Face. So now, I have relaxed MY Hand of protection that I have held steady, but now the world is experiencing what happens when it chooses to reject GOD ALMIGHTY to pursue lesser gods and evil rulers.

There will be a few saved when I remove MY bride, contrary to what many want to believe. Many false teachers want to twist MY Words to appease the people. The people do not want the Truth. They want to touch, feel, and handle the world and their leaders would rather allow them to believe these lies than to place the Truth before them. The people will face the worst because their hearts love evil.

Children, do not listen to the lies you are being fed—you are misled and heading for the broad road to hell if you continue to believe that you can dirty your garments and turn back to the world like Lot's wife. You cannot love the world and your GOD both. MY Ways do not mix with the ways of the world.

Once you start to move to worship the ways of the world, when do you decide you have gone too deep? A little leaven spoils the whole lump. You must pull away—be set apart. Only these will find relief from the evil coming to the world when I return for MY bride, MY pure bride. Seek ME for this purity. Only I can help you distinguish between the ways of the world and MY Ways: only MY SPIRIT indwelling your spirit. There is no other way—not by your power or by your strength—only by the Power of MY HOLY SPIRIT can you conquer the flesh.

Come lay your life at MY Feet. Surrender ALL. It is not too late. Come back to your First LOVE, the ONE WHO Created you. MY Heart waits patiently. Don't tarry. Come with your wrinkled and soiled garment. I will hold you and wipe your tears away. I want to love you—you are kicking against the goads—stop fighting your MAKER, CREATOR. Surrender to ME.

This is your LORD LONGSUFFERING.

Coordinating Scripture:

Matthew 7:21, Not everyone that saith unto ME, LORD, LORD, shall enter into the kingdom of heaven; but he that doeth the will of MY FATHER which is in heaven.

Ephesians 5:6, Let no man deceive you with vain words: for because of these things cometh the wrath of GOD upon the children of disobedience.

Romans 6:23, For the wages of sin is death; but the gift of GOD is eternal life through JESUS CHRIST our LORD.

Zechariah 8:17, And let none of you imagine evil in your hearts against his neighbour; and love no false oath: for all these are things that I hate, saith the LORD.

Galatians 5:9, A little leaven leaveneth the whole lump.

Zechariah 4:6, Then he answered and spake unto me, saying, This is the word of the LORD unto Zerubbabel, saying, Not by might, nor by power, but by MY SPIRIT, saith the LORD of hosts.

Words of the LORD:

"Don't Risk Your Very Soul To The Short-Lived Pursuit Of A Corrupt, Evil World."

(Words Received from Our LORD by Susan, March 5, 2013)

Yes Susan, WE can begin:

Children of the MOST HIGH, I come to you in great distress. There are very few of you who are paying attention to MY Warnings. The world is shifting away from its GOD and you are not taking note. MY people, you seem to think that this obvious shift the world is making

54

toward evil is negligible and it has no true meaning, consequences or that it will lead to any negative ultimate outcome.

You do not know ME or MY Ways if you do not acknowledge that the movement of a world running to evil will not end with a positive outcome. The further the world goes away from MY Holy Ways, the farther down all mankind is spiraling. The evidence of this is clear: wars and rumors of wars; pestilence, men's hearts waxing cold. Soon, darkness will be all encompassing. Truth is becoming a rare commodity. Homes and families are tearing apart. This is only the beginning of what is coming over this earth.

You have a chance to escape the worst that is coming. MY bride will be removed to safety. Only those who have made a full and complete surrender with a sincerely repentant heart, and those who pursue ME with all their heart, soul, mind, and strength will be found ready when the trumpet blows and the church is taken out to safety. Do you want to be among the few who want to go, the few who have rejected the world and its antichrist spirit? This choice is for you to make.

I cannot promise you a spot in MY Heavenlies if you believe for a second chance after I remove the bride: as sudden destruction will come and many will be destroyed following the removal of the church. Don't risk your very soul to the short-lived pursuit of a corrupt, evil world because you can't take your hands off this world and turn to ME. Sadness awaits those who reject ME now. Don't be like Lot's wife…

Choices must be made. Your indecision is a choice. Let ME clean your heart out with MY Blood Covering and by the Truth of MY Word. Come let ME Prepare your heart, purify you so you can shine like gold and you will be able to stand before ME in MY Coming Kingdom. There is no other way to the FATHER but by ME.

Church, your LORD waits patiently for you to desire clean hands and a clean heart so that WE can be together for eternity. Let these Words ring in your ears and infiltrate your hearts.

PATIENCE HAS SPOKEN.

Coordinating Scripture:

Matthew 24:6, And ye shall hear of wars and rumours of wars: see that ye be not troubled: for all these things must come to pass, but the end is not yet.

1 Corinthians 15:52, In a moment, in the twinkling of an eye, at the last trump: for the trumpet shall sound, and the dead shall be raised incorruptible, and we shall be changed.

Matthew 24:12, And because iniquity shall abound, the love of many shall wax cold.

Ephesians 5:26, That HE might sanctify and cleanse it with the washing of water by the word,

John 14:6, JESUS saith unto him, I am the WAY, the TRUTH, and the LIFE: no man cometh unto the FATHER, but by ME.

1 Thessalonians 5:3, For when they shall say, Peace and safety; then sudden destruction cometh upon them, as travail upon a woman with child; and they shall not escape.

CHAPTER 7

The Only Position Of Safety And Well-Being

Is In The Center Of God's Will

Tue, 19 Mar 2013

The LORD's Words:

"This Is The Only Position Of Safety And Well-Being: In The Center Of The Will Of GOD."

GOD's GRACE and MERCY: NOT JUST FOR GOD TO GIVE

LOVE is the greatest WMD: weapon of mass destruction against evil.

LOVE will ultimately annihilate evil.

CHRIST gives grace and mercy freely to those who repent of their sin and surrender their all to HIM. But we are slow to give others this same grace and mercy ourselves. GOD forgives our sins and remembers them no more to our great relief, once we repent and claim the Gift of HIS Blood Ransom paid for us.

We, in turn, are either slow or never forgive others. CHRIST does not hold grudges and throw our old sin up in our faces. It is satan who reminds us of our old forgiven sin, not GOD. We also can't let go of the old sin of others the way we want GOD to forget our ugly pasts.

When we really forgive others and extend to them grace and mercy, unmerited favor—we move them into a place toward understanding CHRIST's Love, freedom from sin, and the pursuit of Truth against the world's ways. We are simultaneously freed from our sinful mindset of unforgiveness, receive the mind of CHRIST, and ultimately the salvation of our own souls.

Make the first move to mend your broken fences. Pursue "forgiving" granting grace and mercy to everyone in your past who has hurt you—whether living or passed away. When I was just a young girl, a close family member was unkind to me and I grew to dislike this person because I was young and hurt. I was so hurt in my heart by this person that I did not even attend their funeral. But when I began to pursue GOD and the views of GOD, I realized I had some unfinished business regarding this individual.

I was alone in my car talking to GOD and I called out to the LORD regarding my sadness over my long-held unforgiveness and hurt. I told the LORD, I could not talk to this person now, but I wanted to forgive them through the LORD. I felt that there was a great burden and barrier between GOD and me that had been lifted at that moment.

Reach for the handle marked "Grace—Mercy—Forgiveness" for all those around you. Release others and yourself to become closer to the LORD.

Yes, it is a narrow way…

Susan Davis

Matthew 18:21-22, 21Then came Peter to HIM, and said, LORD, how oft shall my brother sin against me, and I forgive him? Till seven times? 22JESUS saith unto him, I say not unto thee, Until seven times: but, Until seventy times seven.

Words of the LORD:

"The Lust For The World Is A Distraction The Enemy Has Carefully Plotted Against The People."

(Words Received from Our LORD by Susan, March 11, 2013)

Yes, I have Words for the children:

Children, this is your GOD. I have made you in MY Image. I have forged you from MY Heart. You were made to be in MY Image to be like your GOD, to have MY Characteristics. You have chosen rather to be rebellious, to run far from your GOD. You have blinders on. You are blind guides leading the blind.

I am coming soon for a bride who has made herself ready for ME, her HUSBAND. She must be ready or I cannot take her. Her desire must be for ME—only ME and not for this world. As long as she pursues the world, she is lost, but when she turns back to ME with all her heart, soul, mind, and strength—all these things will be added unto her. I will give all the things she needs to be cared for.

The lust for the world is a distraction the enemy has carefully plotted against the people. This will be their destruction if they don't turn back to ME away from the lust of the world by the plans of MY enemy.

The world is a well-laid trap by MY enemy. He even uses what looks safe and good to entice you away. Only those in MY Will are coming out with ME when I blow the trumpet and call out MY bride. Those who pursue MY Will alone will be found worthy to avoid the death and destruction planned for this evil world.

You can know MY Will by surrendering to it. Stop seeking your own will. Turn and seek MINE. Humble yourself, repent for walking in rebellion apart from the Will of GOD. Bend your knee, lay before ME

59

in humble submission admitting to ME you need your GOD. Until you do this you are MY enemy's to do his will although you can't see it, you are not your own and you are working for the enemy, working against MY Kingdom, rebelling against your GOD CREATOR, and heading down the broad road to hell with the vast majority of humanity. Only when you turn off this wide road to the narrow path by coming into MY Will by your own humble submission, will you be saved from eternal damnation.

This is your choice to make. All are given a choice. Choose ME as your LORD and MASTER and find life everlasting. Come to know ME as worthy of your choosing. I am the FRIEND WHO never leaves, the LOVE WHO never forgets. I am the FATHER WHO never rejects. I am the ROCK. Come to know ME as your own.

The world is rejecting its GOD. Don't be left behind when I remove the few who pursue ME with all their heart. Turn to ME and see the Truth.

The LAMB…The LION.

Coordinating Scripture:

Genesis 1:27, So GOD created man in HIS OWN Image, in the Image of GOD created HE him; male and female created HE them.

Romans 5:12, Wherefore, as by one man sin entered into the world, and death by sin; and so death passed upon all men, for that all have sinned:

Luke 13:24-27, 24Strive to enter in at the strait gate: for many, I say unto you, will seek to enter in, and shall not be able.25When once the MASTER of the house is risen up, and hath shut to the door, and ye begin to stand without, and to knock at the door, saying,

LORD, LORD, open unto us; and HE shall answer and say unto you, I know you not whence ye are: 26Then shall ye begin to say, We have eaten and drunk in THY Presence, and THOU hast taught in our streets. 27But HE shall say, I tell you, I know you not whence ye are; depart from ME, all ye workers of iniquity.

Matthew 7:21-23, 21Not everyone that saith unto ME, LORD, LORD, shall enter into the kingdom of heaven; but he that doeth the Will of MY FATHER which is in heaven. 22Many will say to ME in that day, LORD, LORD, have we not prophesied in THY Name? And in THY Name have cast out devils? And in THY Name done many wonderful works? 23And then will I profess unto them, I never knew you: depart from ME, ye that work iniquity.

Words of the LORD:

"This Is The Only Position Of Safety And Well-Being: In The Center Of The Will Of GOD."

(Words Received from Our LORD by Susan, March 12, 2013)

I will give you the Words—We can begin:

Children, it is your GOD. I dwell in High Places. I am EVERYWHERE. MY Name is LIGHT. I am ALL ENCOMPASSING. You cannot comprehend ME. Your human mind cannot grasp WHO I AM.

I am EVERYTHING YOU HAVE EVER WANTED in your GOD CREATOR. I can Meet ALL your needs as a human. I created you with needs so that you might turn to ME, seek ME, and find ME to provide for you the needs of your longing human heart.

You have run from your GOD. All have gone astray. All needs can be met through ME, yet you look elsewhere to be satisfied and you die in your filth apart from ME. Very few seek ME and find ME. Only a handful find ME in the way I want to be found. I do not want a partial finding.

Many take portions of ME and believe themselves full. They are still seeking from the world for the things I, GOD, can provide entirely. Empty-handed, lost—these are MY children. I came to earth as a human to FILL, to give life abundantly. I died so many could be filled—filled with MY Love, Wholeness, Peace, and Comfort—to be right in the center of GOD's Will.

This is the only position of safety and well-being: in the center of the Will of GOD. Apart from this, there is no peace, wholeness, or security. If you do not find yourself in the center of MY Will, you will be lost for all eternity.

It is not too late to make your way to safety to be ready for MY Return for the bride, but you must choose to surrender your ALL to ME. Ask for MY SPIRIT to FULLY indwell your spirit. You must desire to be completely filled with MY SPIRIT, walking in MY Ways, moving in MY Truth. This is the only safe route—the narrow path.

Adorn yourself with the beauty of MY SPIRIT, MY Truth, MY Will. Only this will make your garments clean and ready. Only with MY SPIRIT can MY Word come to life for you. Wash in MY Blood, open yourself up to MY SPIRIT, relax your grip on a lost and dying world.

Turn back to GOD: GOD WHO Created you for MY Pleasure. Come walk in the path I have laid before you. All other paths and walks lead to destruction apart from the ONE WAY GOD Meant for you to go. Come let ME Lead you—take your hand.

I am SAFE, SURE, and FOUNDED.

I AM THE CHIEF CORNER STONE

Coordinating Scripture:

1 John 1:5, This then is the message which we have heard of him, and declare unto you, that GOD is LIGHT, and in HIM is no darkness at all.

James 1:17, Every good gift and every perfect gift is from above, and cometh down from the FATHER of lights, with WHOM is no variableness, neither shadow of turning.

Romans 3:23, For all have sinned, and come short of the Glory of GOD;

Revelation 3:16, So then because thou art lukewarm, and neither cold nor hot, I will spue thee out of my mouth.

Psalm 147:11, The LORD taketh pleasure in them that fear HIM, in those that hope in HIS mercy.

Luke 20:17, And HE beheld them, and said, What is this then that is written, The STONE which the builders rejected, the same is become the HEAD of the corner?

Ephesians 2:20, And are built upon the foundation of the apostles and prophets, JESUS CHRIST HIMSELF being the CHIEF CORNER STONE;

Wed, 27 Mar 2013

The LORD's Words:

"I Am Calling You Out: Be Separate From This Evil World..."

There are three things you need to be aware of to be ready for the LORD's Return in the rapture of the bride—the true church in these, the end times:

a) You need to be watching—only those watching will be ready. This scripture tells why: Matthew 24:42-44, Watch therefore: for ye know not what hour your LORD doth come. 43But know this, that if the goodman of the house had known in what watch the thief would come, he would have watched, and would not have suffered his house to be broken up. 44Therefore be ye also ready: for in such an hour as ye think not the SON of man cometh. Matthew is clear that without watching, the goodman will be caught off guard and not ready and if you aren't ready then you won't be taken. So "watching" which means to keep your focus on the LORD is essential to being ready. Luke 17:32 says: Remember Lot's wife. Lot's wife turned back to the world. If you are turning back to the world and not watching for the LORD, remember Lot's wife—she did not have a good ending and you won't either.

b) You need to be in the FATHER's Will—only those FULLY surrendered to the LORD, giving HIM everything, will be ready: This scripture tells why: Matthew 7:21-23, 21Not everyone that saith unto ME, LORD, LORD, shall enter into the kingdom of heaven; but he that doeth the Will of MY FATHER WHICH is in heaven. 22Many will say to ME in that day, LORD, LORD, have we not prophesied in THY Name? And in THY Name have cast out devils? And in THY

Name done many wonderful works? 23And then will I profess unto them, I never knew you: depart from ME, ye that work iniquity.

c) You need to be fully baptized in and consumed by the HOLY SPIRIT—only those with a FULL OIL LAMP will be ready: In this scripture the LORD revealed to me that many who say they received a filling of the HOLY SPIRIT when they accepted CHRIST and don't believe in a separate baptism of the HOLY SPIRIT are misled. Water baptism and HOLY SPIRIT baptism are two separate events from receiving CHRIST as your SAVIOR and the HOLY SPIRIT baptism required by GOD to be rapture ready is a separate event.

This is what the LORD showed me about Paul (also Saul in this passage below) and his baptism in the HOLY SPIRIT event. Paul was on the road to Damascus and he had an encounter with CHRIST: Acts 9:3-18, And as he journeyed, he came near Damascus: and suddenly there shined round about him a light from heaven: 4And he fell to the earth, and heard a Voice saying unto him, Saul, Saul, why persecutest thou ME? 5And he said, WHO art THOU, LORD? And the LORD said, I am JESUS whom thou persecutest: it is hard for thee to kick against the pricks. 6And he trembling and astonished said, LORD, what wilt thou have me to do?

At this point, there is no question that Paul met CHRIST supernaturally and acknowledges HIM as his LORD and MASTER because he asks HIM what the LORD wants him to do and then as a new follower and believer of CHRIST, Paul does as he is commanded, but HE IS STILL NOT SPIRIT-FILLED AS CHRIST'S NEW FOLLOWER:

And the LORD said unto him, Arise, and go into the city, and it shall be told thee what thou must do. 7And the men which journeyed with him stood speechless, hearing a voice, but seeing no man. 8And Saul arose from the earth; and when his eyes were opened, he saw no man: but they led him by the hand, and brought him into Damascus. 9 And he was three days without sight, and neither did eat nor drink.

And the LORD instructs Ananias in Damascus to pray over the new follower Paul to be baptized in the HOLY SPIRIT:

10And there was a certain disciple at Damascus, named Ananias; and to him said the LORD in a vision, Ananias. And he said, Behold, I am here, LORD. 11And the LORD said unto him, Arise, and go into the street which is called Straight, and enquire in the house of Judas for one called Saul, of Tarsus: for, behold, he prayeth, 12And hath seen in a vision a man named Ananias coming in, and putting his hand on him, that he might receive his sight. 13Then Ananias answered, LORD, I have heard by many of this man, how much evil he hath done to THY saints at Jerusalem: 14And here he hath authority from the chief priests to bind all that call on THY Name. 15But the LORD said unto him, Go thy way: for he is a chosen vessel unto ME, to bear MY Name before the Gentiles, and kings, and the children of Israel: 16For I will shew him how great things he must suffer for MY Name's sake. 17And Ananias went his way, and entered into the house; and putting his hands on him said, Brother Saul, the LORD, even JESUS, that appeared unto thee in the way as thou camest, hath sent me, that thou mightest receive thy sight, and be filled with the HOLY GHOST. 18And immediately there fell from his eyes as it had been scales: and he received sight forthwith, and arose, and was baptized.

It was at this point that Paul is FILLED WITH THE HOLY SPIRIT AND NOT BEFORE. The scales fell off his eyes and he could begin the work the LORD was giving him to do. (Also note they were in Ananias' house so this was clearly NOT a water baptism—it was a baptism of the HOLY SPIRIT—separate from water baptism and separate from acknowledging CHRIST as SAVIOR as a new follower.) Are you baptized in the HOLY SPIRIT? For more scripture on the baptism of the HOLY SPIRIT also read Acts 19:1-7!

Words of the LORD:

"I Am Calling You Out: Be Separate From This Evil World That Runs Apart From GOD."

(Words Received from Our LORD by Susan, March 22, 2013)

Daughter, let ME begin to give you Words:

The hour is late children. MY Coming is forth coming, nigh. Do you not see the writing on the wall? Do you not see the messages I am sending all around you? Not just Words through MY messengers, but through the skies, through the rumors of wars escalating, through the evil growing among men, through the weather, through the rumblings around MY covenant land Israel. These are all signs that time is running out.

I have sent dreams and visions and poured out MY SPIRIT on mankind. The warnings have been clear and sure. I sent MY Word ahead, so you would know what to look for. MY Prophecies are all coming to pass. You are now seeing the onset of a great move of MY SPIRIT over the earth: both to show forth HIS Greatness and to pull away to expose evil. Evil is birthing in all four points of the globe

67

as I lift MY Protective Hand. This is the result of man rejecting GOD in all his ways.

Men are seeking answers through all means, but through their GOD, CREATOR. Men are running to evil means for solutions to their deepest questions about their lives, their futures, their well-being, their security. This is evil as men handle everything under the son but to pursue ME, their ALL IN ALL.

I am absolutely THE SOLUTION to all the longings of the human heart. I hold the key to every care and concern a man has about his life. I know all—I am ALL! But men refuse to pursue ME and MY treasure trove of solutions. I possess ALL knowledge and understanding. I AM the EVERLASTING LIGHT, The ETERNAL TORCH WHO Leads the way.

Soon, I am coming to claim MY beloved: the church, who I died for who I am coming to rescue to place in MY eternal rest as MY everlasting companion. This is MY reward and the joy set before ME. Come join ME. Meet ME in the sky.

I am calling you out: be separate from this evil world that runs apart from GOD. Stop searching for answers from a world that is crumbling and coming undone. Now is the time to surrender to ME and come to your senses. Awaken, let the scales fall off your eyes as MY Son Paul did. Let ME change your heart and renew your mind. I can do it. I am willing!

Run like you have never run before to your GOD, SAVIOR!

This is the MESSIAH,

KING of kings...LORD of lords...ALL in all.

Coordinating Scripture:

Luke 21:25, And there shall be signs in the sun, and in the moon, and in the stars; and upon the earth distress of nations, with perplexity; the sea and the waves roaring;

Matthew 24:6, And ye shall hear of wars and rumours of wars: see that ye be not troubled: for all these things must come to pass, but the end is not yet.

Matthew 24:12, And because iniquity shall abound, the love of many shall wax cold.

Zechariah 12:2, Behold, I will make Jerusalem a cup of trembling unto all the people round about, when they shall be in the siege both against Judah and against Jerusalem.

Joel 2:28, And it shall come to pass afterward, that I will pour out my spirit upon all flesh; and your sons and your daughters shall prophesy, your old men shall dream dreams, your young men shall see visions:

2 Peter 1:21, For the prophecy came not in old time by the will of man: but holy men of GOD spake as they were moved by the HOLY GHOST.

Isaiah 31:1, Woe to them that go down to Egypt for help; and stay on horses, and trust in chariots, because they are many; and in horsemen, because they are very strong; but they look not unto the HOLY ONE of Israel, neither seek the Lord!

Acts 9:17-18, And Ananias went his way, and entered into the house; and putting his hands on him said, Brother Saul, the LORD, even JESUS, that appeared unto thee in the way as thou camest, hath sent me, that thou mightest receive thy sight, and be filled with the HOLY GHOST. 18 And immediately there fell from his eyes as it had been scales: and he received sight forthwith, and arose, and was baptized.

Words of the LORD:

"Few Discover I Am A GOD WHO Is Just And Will Judge According To Each Individual's Relationship With ME In This Life."

(Words Received from Our LORD by Susan, March 23, 2013)

Take down these Words:

There is an overwhelming belief that I am not coming soon: so many want to believe otherwise. This world is too attractive to them— longing and looking for MY Coming is the last thing on their minds.

When I come to bring out MY church, I will only be looking for a ready bride—a church perched in anticipation of her coming KING. I am coming in ALL MY Glory. Only those waiting...ready...watching with their robes white and stain-free will come out of this stagnant world—a cesspool of evil, a stench under MY Nose.

Pin your hopes on the LIVING GOD. This is the ONE True Path—all others lead to destruction. The world is in a rapid descent to ultimate immorality and decay. Once I take out MY bride—MY true worshipful followers, this world will cave in on itself under the weight of the evil that will consume the land.

There will be bloodshed, cruelty, abominable atrocities. Man will enter a never witnessed before level of ultimate degradation. Children who turn back to ME after I take MY church out will find themselves under the rule of a cruel tyrant world leader: the

70

antichrist, who will round up the true believers, the ones who turn back to their GOD in great remorse. Theirs will be a sad plight as they must then endure the worst possible torment, torture, and death for their decision to return to their LORD and to reject the antichrist system.

Horror awaits MY left behind, lukewarm church who must do the hard things to return to their GOD. Many will not be willing to pay the price before them in order to obtain their eternal freedom. Those who choose against ME for the antichrist system will lose their place with ME for eternity and they will be tormented for eternity instead.

Hard choices must be made by those who are left and refuse to follow ME now. Turn to ME now. Surrender your ALL. Lay your life down. I am ready to take you out with ME when I come for MY beautiful bride.

Scoffers, mockers, doubters, lovers of this evil world will soon learn the error of their wayward ways turning back away from their GOD to give themselves over to seducing spirits and evil longings. They are grasping at evil pursuits following their own self-made paths believing they know best for themselves apart from their MAKER GOD WHO first loved them, created them, gave them life. Woe to those who believe this world a better choice than the LIVING GOD WHO makes all, WHO is ALL in all.

Come back to your senses lost church. Your love for ME is weak, your heart is failing, you have no temperature, you have grown cold. I cannot take you with ME, if you believe yourself ready while you devote yourself to this evil world. You are deceived, lost, and your destination is the broad road where many travel to, lost for eternity, everlasting hell.

If this Word sounds untrue, it is because you have not spent time in MY Word or getting to know ME. If MY lost children would come to fear ME, then they would come back to the narrow road and separate themselves from the world and evil.

Few discover I am a GOD WHO is just and will judge according to each individual's relationship with ME in this life. Do you know your GOD? Come know ME before it is too late. MY Warnings are coming to pass. Do not find yourself outside MY Will, lost for eternity. MY adversary is cruel.

Your choice is before your face. I am the ETERNAL OMNIPRESENT GOD. Reach out. I stand before you.

Coordinating Scripture:

Matthew 24:43, But know this, that if the goodman of the house had known in what watch the thief would come, he would have watched, and would not have suffered his house to be broken up.

1 John 2:22, Who is a liar but he that denieth that JESUS is the CHRIST? He is antichrist, that denieth the FATHER and the SON.

Revelation 7:9, After this I beheld, and, lo, a great multitude, which no man could number, of all nations, and kindreds, and people, and tongues, stood before the throne, and before the Lamb, clothed with white robes, and palms in their hands;

Revelation 7:13-14, 13And one of the elders answered, saying unto me, What are these which are arrayed in white robes? and whence came they? 14And I said unto him, Sir, thou knowest. And he said to me, These are they which came out of great tribulation, and have washed their robes, and made them white in the blood of the LAMB.

Jude 1:17-19, 17But, beloved, remember ye the words which were spoken before of the apostles of our LORD JESUS CHRIST; 18How that they told you there should be mockers in the last time, who should walk after their own ungodly lusts. 19These be they who separate themselves, sensual, having not the SPIRIT.

CHAPTER 8

Come To Know ME As Your FIRST LOVE

Fri, 5 Apr 2013

The LORD's Words:

"Come To Know ME As Your FIRST LOVE."

2 Peter 3:3-4, 3Knowing this first, that there shall come in the last days scoffers, walking after their own lusts, 4And saying, Where is the promise of HIS coming? For since the fathers fell asleep, all things continue as they were from the beginning of the creation.

Definition Scoffers/Mockers: someone who jeers or mocks or treats something with contempt or calls out in derision.

It is perplexing how so many who claim to be "Christian" really just don't believe the Bible they profess to live by. How many Christians "edit" the Bible in their minds to suit their own tastes and lifestyles?

One BIG chunk of copy that the lukewarm Christians like to delete out of their personal Bibles is anything to do with the coming rapture and subsequent tribulation. If they hear from people who are trying to tell them that the Bible is coming together NOW with record precision, they just do not want to hear about it. (This is also Bible prophecy coming to pass…)

Really if you think about it—it's kind of humorous when you consider the number of people who sit in churches every week, carry Bibles around with them, and profess with stalwart certainty to believe in the entire Bible, and imagine if you will, how these same people would have reacted to people from actual Bible times. If these same people living today lived in the time of Noah, they would have declared him eccentric and downright crazy building a boat in a desert region where floods are unheard of...would you have persecuted Noah?

Or what about Ezekiel—if he came to you today with his Biblical description of seeing GOD's Throne Room, would you think he needed to seek psychiatric counseling? Ezekiel 10:11-13, 11When they went, they went upon their four sides; they turned not as they went, but to the place whither the head looked they followed it; they turned not as they went. 12And their whole body, and their backs, and their hands, and their wings, and the wheels, were full of eyes round about, even the wheels that they four had. 13As for the wheels, it was cried unto them in my hearing, O wheel.

How about Isaiah and his description of seeing the seraphim in the Throne Room of GOD? Would you think him crazy if he told you his story today? Isaiah 6:1-3, In the year that King Uzziah died, I saw also the LORD sitting upon a throne, high and lifted up, and HIS Train filled the temple. 2 Above it stood the seraphims: each one had six wings; with twain he covered his face, and with twain he covered his feet, and with twain he did fly. 3 And one cried unto another, and said, Holy, holy, holy, is the LORD of hosts: the whole earth is full of HIS Glory.

How about Mary, the Mother of CHRIST? Would you be the first in line to talk behind her back about what kind of crazy person says she is pregnant by the power of GOD? Would you have been one of the first to denounce her claims or ridicule her for telling such a farfetched story?

And what of CHRIST HIMSELF? Would you have been so accepting of HIS Story? When HE said: "To be MY disciple you must eat MY Body and drink MY Blood?" Would you have walked away? Even HIS own family and friends called HIM crazy—would you have chimed in with them? Mark 3:21, And when HIS friends heard of it, they went out to lay hold on HIM: for they said, HE is beside HIMSELF. Would you have called for HIM to be crucified?

The stories that you have taught your own children or you, yourself have learned and believed in Sunday School—YOU, LUKEWARM CHURCH, WOULD HAVE PERSECUTED YESTERDAY'S BIBLE CHARACTERS.

So just what DO YOU BELIEVE? Do you believe the signs GOD gave to be watching for HIS Return that have now all come to pass signaling for you to be ready for the LORD's rapture of HIS bride—the true church? Or have you torn those pages out of your Bible because you like the world too much and the idea that the LORD is coming soon messes with your own personal will, desires, and pursuits? Well, you can't have it both ways: you either love the world OR GOD and if you love the world then the love of the FATHER is not in you…

1 John 2:15, Love not the world, neither the things that are in the world. If any man love the world, the love of the FATHER is not in him.

Words of the LORD:

"The More The World Rejects ME, The More I Will Lift My Hand Of Protection."

(Words Received from Our LORD by Susan, March 29, 2013)

Susan, it is I, your LORD, ready to give you new Words:

MY children the hour is closing in for MY return. I am coming and no one can stop ME. There is nothing that can stop GOD from accomplishing what HE plans to do. Everything you see is coming to pass because I ordain it. It is MY Plan. I am allowing the evil in the world commensurate with the rejection of GOD. The more the world rejects ME, the more I will lift my hand of protection. This is no different from what I have done in the past. When MY children reject ME, they experience the error of their ways.

MY children, you will reject your GOD and then you will experience being controlled by MY enemy. He will take over you because I will release you to him after MY church is removed in the coming rapture. You will be consumed by great evil.

These words are not empty promises. Already you can see the enemy has a toehold. And soon he will be taking over as the greatest tyrant the world has ever seen. There is no one who will be safe who challenges his dictatorship. And those who fall into his plans from fear will be ostracized from ME for eternity.

After the church is removed, the choices for the people to make will be very difficult. Many will just run into the arms of the enemy, thinking he has all the answers. Others, who know better, will be penalized unto death: to make their way back to their GOD. It will not be an easy route, as MY enemy will not make them go down easily.

Suicide will not be an answer for you either. So don't even consider it. Although many will take their own lives thinking this is the safest escape route, suicide is not the answer as you do not have the right to even take your own life. This life is MINE to give and MINE to take. I am the GIVER and TAKER of ALL life. I am even in control of the evil that takes life.

Now is the time to decide for your GOD. Press into ME, run to ME, lay your life down before ME. I paid the price on a cruel cross. I paid your penalty. Now you can be saved and given new life. You can avoid the atrocities that are coming.

The world will be dark beyond your imagination. Make yourself ready to avoid this pain and suffering. Wash in MY Blood and let ME Prepare your garments. MY Love and Grace is available now, but soon I will pull away MY Extended Hand and use it to Carry MY bride off to safety, and those who are left will find out what it is to reject their GOD. These words are true. The sand in the hourglass is shifting.

I am your GOD. I Humbled MYSELF in a way you cannot imagine. If you reject this Great Offer of Love that I extend to you, then I cannot help but reject you for eternity. Let these Words ring in your ears.

This is your GOD, GREAT and POWERFUL,

YAHUSHUA.

Coordinating Scripture:

Jeremiah 6:19, Hear, O earth: behold, I will bring evil upon this people, even the fruit of their thoughts, because they have not hearkened unto MY Words, nor to MY Law, but rejected it.

1 John 2:18, Little children, it is the last time: and as ye have heard that antichrist shall come, even now are there many antichrists; whereby we know that it is the last time.

Revelation 14:11, And the smoke of their torment ascendeth up forever and ever: and they have no rest day nor night, who worship the beast and his image, and whosoever receiveth the mark of his name.

Job 33:4, The SPIRIT of GOD hath made me, and the Breath of the ALMIGHTY hath given me life.

1 Samuel 2:6, The LORD killeth, and maketh alive: HE bringeth down to the grave, and bringeth up.

Words of the LORD:

"Come To Know ME As Your FIRST LOVE."

(Words Received from Our LORD by Susan, March 31, 2013)

Daughter, I can give you a letter. This is for the people, those who want to listen:

Children, I am your GOD. Only few actually acknowledge ME, the way I want to be acknowledged.

I want to be your ALL in all. I want to be your FIRST LOVE, your BEGINNING, your ENDING, your FIRST THOUGHT each day and your LAST THOUGHT at the close of each day. I want to be more important to you than the pull of the world: to be loved with ALL your heart, soul, and strength.

I want FIRST PLACE. I don't want to follow behind your financial pursuits, your spouse, your children, the things of the world that draw you away from ME. I don't even want to be second to your church programs and the things you believe represent ME. Even these are distractions that keep us from being close. All the busyness in the world you do in MY Name means nothing if you don't know ME, truly know ME.

Come to know ME as your FIRST LOVE. Make ME the ONE you live for: your LORD and MASTER. This is why you were created. Apart from this directive, you are outside MY Will for your life and lost…

MY Kingdom will consist of those who lay this life down, put ME above all else, pursue MY Ways, read to understand MY Words, and seek ME for ALL their answers. These are they who will accompany ME when I come to remove MY bride, MY church, who will be with ME for eternity.

Consider these Words seriously. They are serious Words. All other directives for your life will not lead you to the NARROW PATH, the way this truth will and outside of MY NARROW Way you will be lost on the broad road that most people take. The broad road leads to hell, torment, and eternally apart from your GOD, the Only SOURCE of Love, Hope, and Well-being.

Come and seek the NARROW WAY. Surrender your ALL. Seek MY Face. I AM the ONLY WAY by which all men can come to the FATHER.

I AM the MESSIAH,

YAHUSHUA.

Coordinating Scripture:

Luke 10:27, And HE answering said, Thou shalt love the LORD THY GOD with all thy heart, and with all thy soul, and with all thy strength, and with all thy mind; and thy neighbour as thyself.

Revelation 2:4, Nevertheless I have somewhat against thee, because thou hast left thy FIRST LOVE.

Mark 10:25, It is easier for a camel to go through the eye of a needle, than for a rich man to enter into the Kingdom of GOD.

Matthew 8:21-22, And another of HIS disciples said unto HIM, LORD, suffer me first to go and bury my father. 22But JESUS said unto him, Follow ME; and let the dead bury their dead.

Matthew 7:21-23, 21Not everyone that saith unto ME, LORD, LORD, shall enter into the Kingdom of Heaven; but he that doeth the Will of MY FATHER which is in Heaven. 22Many will say to ME in that day, LORD, LORD, have we not prophesied in THY Name? And in THY Name have cast out devils? And in THY Name done many wonderful works? 23And then will I profess unto them, I never knew you: depart from ME, ye that work iniquity.

John 14:6, JESUS saith unto him, I am the WAY, the TRUTH, and the LIFE: no man cometh unto the FATHER, but by ME.

Fri, 19 Apr 2013

Words of the LORD:

"I Cannot Allow You To Enter MY Kingdom As Long As You Desire To Pursue The World."

(Words Received from Our LORD by Susan, April 8, 2013)

Yes Susan, I can give you Words:

MY children, I am GOD. You have been watching for ME, if you are MY loyal church. For this I am pleased. MY bride longs for MY Coming. She watches the skies. She looks longingly for her GOD to break through the clouds to call her up hither.

I am a GOD WHO longs to be with MY children—those who lay everything down for their GOD—all the earthly delights that pull away MY lukewarm church who know ME not: MY lukewarm church who believe they know ME, but really don't. They fill ME in between the cracks of their lives. They put ME below all their other pursuits. They think of ME only when they need their GOD they believe—only when their lives are in crisis, when they have serious needs. Everyday is serious, O' lukewarm church. You delude yourself if you believe you are able to run your life apart from your GOD.

You are heading down the broad road to hell because you have chosen against ME in favor of running things your own way, in your own will. It's not really your will—it is MY enemy's will, but deception is the greatest tool MY enemy uses to captivate MY children and lure them into hell.

Waken O' lukewarm. You are no match for MY enemy and his deception and lies. Unless you are fully surrendered and in the Will of your GOD, the enemy has you under his control to do damage in MY Kingdom. You will be judged as guilty of high treason against your GOD and the Kingdom of Heaven if you come before ME without MY Forgiveness, outside of MY Will, apart from MY Blood Covering, and the ransom I paid for you on the cross where I gave MY Life.

Children, rethink your decisions and choices you make against your GOD in favor of MY enemy. You will be held accountable. I cannot allow you to enter MY Kingdom as long as you desire to pursue the world. I am a JEALOUS GOD. Do not wait to change your heart. Your decision may come too late. There are serious consequences for those who handle MY HOLY Words and then reject them.

Turn your life over to ME BEFORE it is too late. Many would have you believe that you do not need to watch for your GOD. These are liars who twist MY Words because they love the world and the devil their father who they serve. Don't be deceived. WATCH BECAUSE you do not know the hour I will return. Most will be left behind because the enemy will deceive them and they will know then how wrong their thinking was.

It will be just as in the days of Noah and the multitude will be caught unaware, off guard, left to an evil outcome. Get ready now, you must make ready and to tell those around you so you can be the hands and feet of your GOD.

Turn your heart toward the Coming BRIDEGROOM,

I AM HE,

YAHUSHUA HA MASHIACH.

Coordinating Scripture:

2 Timothy 4:8, Henceforth there is laid up for me a crown of righteousness, which the LORD, the RIGHTEOUS JUDGE, shall give me at that day: and not to me only, but unto all them also that love HIS appearing.

1 Thessalonians 4:17, Then we which are alive and remain shall be caught up together with them in the clouds, to meet the LORD in the air: and so shall we ever be with the LORD.

Matthew 24:42, Watch therefore: for ye know not what hour your LORD doth come.

Matthew 24:38-39, 38For as in the days that were before the flood they were eating and drinking, marrying and giving in marriage, until the day that Noah entered into the ark, 39And knew not until the flood came, and took them all away; so shall also the coming of the SON of man be.

Words of the LORD:

"Many, Many Have Come And Gone Before You, Thinking They Could Cheat Death And Hell, But To No Avail."

(Words Received from Our LORD by Susan, April 9, 2013)

Yes MY daughter, I will give Words for the people:

Children of the MOST HIGH GOD:

Your lives are in the balance—you believe that time is on your side and that you control your own destiny. Many, many have come and gone before you, thinking they could cheat death and hell but to no avail.

There is only ONE WAY to cheat hell out of your presence and that is MY Way through MY Will—GOD's Will: only by a FULL surrender of your life over to ME.

What is full surrender, you are wondering? It is falling to your knees, repenting of your sin with remorse over living out of rebellion in front of your GOD, choosing sin instead of righteousness. It is turning your life over to GOD for MY Use, for MY Glory, and to reach others for the Kingdom.

Partial surrender, clinging to your own will is not complete submission. This takes place daily, surrendering your will to ME everyday, giving up your long range, future plans which are always outside of MY Will.

Your ways are not MY Ways, your thoughts are not MY Thoughts. I know the beginning from the end. I know the outcome before you make your plans. Put your hope and trust in ME. I AM ALL KNOWING, ALL SEEING, ALL POWERFUL. I am the BEGINNING and the END.

Why question your trust in an ALL KNOWING GOD? Come, know your GOD, CREATOR. Get to know ME through MY Book, MY Words, through talking with ME. Come to know I can be trusted. MY Ways are infinitely better than your ways.

I am coming for a pure bride, to rescue her from coming destruction. Come now and get fitted for your wedding garments: white robes of righteousness, purity, wrinkle-free—without spot or stain. Only I can fit you for these garments; make you ready; clean your heart. This is MY desire.

I am standing ready to receive you to leave when I come for MY ready church who watches eagerly for the BRIDEGROOM. Be among the few who look past the attraction of the world and its cheap thrills. Come to Real, Lasting Love: your GOD, the LOVER of your soul.

LOVE is Coming! Don't miss the BRIDEGROOM when HE Appears.

I am only coming for ready hearts.

SAVIOR of all mankind,

KING of kings,

GOD of the universe.

Coordinating Scripture:

Matthew 7:21, Not everyone that saith unto ME, LORD, LORD, shall enter into the kingdom of heaven; but he that doeth the Will of MY FATHER which is in heaven.

Isaiah 55:9, For, as the heavens are higher than the earth, so are MY Ways higher than your ways, and MY Thoughts than your thoughts.

Revelation 1:8, I am ALPHA and OMEGA, The BEGINNING and the ENDING, saith the LORD, which IS, and which WAS, and which IS TO COME, the ALMIGHTY.

Genesis 35:2, Then Jacob said unto his household, and to all that were with him, Put away the strange gods that are among you, and be clean, and change your garments:

Revelation 16:15, Behold, I come as a thief. Blessed is he that watcheth, and keepeth his garments, lest he walk naked, and they see his shame.

Tue, 30 Apr 2013

The LORD's Words:

"The World Is Crumbling Because It Is Distancing Itself From GOD."

Have you ever been "fired" from a job? When you are fired or lose a job you will feel the immediate sting of the loss. It is devastating and overwhelming.

Daily people who die are being "let go" by GOD for all eternity and sent to hell to face torment, torture, and separation from GOD and all that is good. Your ultimate termination from GOD's Eternal Presence and heaven can be avoided.

Here are GOD's prerequisites for avoiding eternal damnation in exchange for our earthly rebellion before a Holy GOD:

-Repent of your sin to a Holy GOD.

-Surrender your all and your own will to CHRIST, even your future life and acknowledge CHRIST as your SAVIOR by the Power of HIS Blood and HIS Name and by the ransom HE paid for you on a cross 2,000 years ago.

-Ask the LORD to fill you with the HOLY SPIRIT and to give you a full oil lamp.

-Read your Bible daily and ask for the HOLY SPIRIT to reveal Truth in the words to your heart.

-Talk to GOD all day. Let HIM be your moment by moment GUIDE, TEACHER, BEST FRIEND, and LOVER of your soul.

Words of the LORD:

"The World Is Crumbling Because It Is Distancing Itself From GOD."

(Words Received from Our LORD by Susan, April 21, 2013)

Words from the LORD:

There is an hour coming of great desolation to the world. It is arising. It can be seen. The people are beginning to see it. Yes, in their spirits they know it is true. They are living in denial—they do not want to face it.

The world is changing and they do not want to face it. It is just as I have said it would be. MY Book has been clear. I have laid out the Truth in advance. I have been clear and MY Words are coming to pass. The world is crumbling because it is distancing itself from GOD.

The hour is coming when Truth is hard to find. Truth is becoming more and more difficult to find. It is being replaced by lies of the enemy. He is coming in behind the missing Truth and replacing it with his lies. And the people are falling for it. They love to hear what tickles their ears: it doesn't matter what they are hearing—and that they are going to hell.

They just want their stiff necked ways. They just want to rebel against their GOD in favor of playing with the world. People all over the world are committing adultery against ME. They are sleeping with the enemy. They are playing with every pagan god and pagan belief that they can get their hands on.

MY Truth is not desirable because it pulls their sins too much into the Light and the people want to stay in the dark where they can rebel against their GOD. Very few want to read MY Word. They believe what they don't know won't, hurt them. But if they read MY Word, they will see that they will be held accountable for every sin they commit in this life and that they need a SAVIOR. I AM HE, I AM that SAVIOR. Only by accepting the ransom I paid for you, will your sin be covered when you face ME... and you WILL FACE ME. ALL men will face their GOD and give accountability for their life. Will you have your stains and sin cleared by MY Blood Ransom or will you come before ME empty handed and hell bound?

Your life of sin will be judged by a Holy GOD as guilty and the only thing that will clear your name will be the acceptance of the debt I paid for you on the Cross of Calvary. This is the only thing acceptable in MY Court. There is a choice to make. It is your choice to make and time is running out. Choose who you will serve: your GOD, CREATOR, or MY enemy. The outcome is your choice to make.

Let these Words stand as a warning to all who read them.

This is GOD ALMIGHTY,

JUDGE of all men.

Coordinating Scripture:

2 Timothy 4:3-4, For the time will come when they will not endure sound doctrine; but after their own lusts shall they heap to themselves teachers, having itching ears; And they shall turn away their ears from the truth, and shall be turned unto fables.

Mark 8:38, Whosoever therefore shall be ashamed of ME and of MY Words in this adulterous and sinful generation; of him also shall the SON of man be ashamed, when HE cometh in the Glory of HIS FATHER with the holy angels.

John 8:12, Then spake JESUS again unto them, saying, I am the LIGHT of the world: he that followeth ME shall not walk in darkness, but shall have the light of life.

John 3:19, And this is the condemnation, that LIGHT is come into the world, and men loved darkness rather than LIGHT, because their deeds were evil.

Romans 14:12, So then every one of us shall give account of himself to GOD.

Genesis 18:25, That be far from thee to do after this manner, to slay the righteous with the wicked: and that the righteous should be as the wicked, that be far from thee: Shall not the JUDGE of all the earth do right?

CHAPTER 9

I Am Coming To Retrieve Only Those Who Are In MY Will

Words of the LORD:

"I Am Coming To Retrieve Only Those Who Are In MY Will."

(Words Received from Our LORD by Susan, April 23, 2013)

Yes it is I, your LORD. I am ready to give you Words:

Today children, I want to address you with new Words, Words that will make you sit up and listen: I am coming to retrieve only those who are in MY Will: MY Perfect Will. All others will be left back to face the worst atrocities and events.

So few are listening and paying attention. They are succumbing to the wiles of the devil. He places blinders on all he controls. Ask yourself if you have the same scales on your eyes that MY son Paul had before he encountered ME on the Road to Damascus? Are you blinded to Truth? Blinders come in many forms. Sin will blind you— willful sin against ME, your GOD. Riches, wealth, and fame will take down those in this world.

I am a needy GOD desiring your full attention. If you are clutching the world, you will not find ME. The world will be the only thing you see. One day, I will come and take MY ready bride and if you are holding the world tightly to yourself, your hands will be too full for ME to pull you out to safety. Let go of this evil, failing, crumbling world. Stop longing and lusting over it and all it stands for: it is an enmity to ME, your GOD. Drop this world and turn to run to ME, your GOD SAVIOR and Coming BRIDEGROOM of Eternity.

This world will soon fall into evil hands and be consumed by evil after MY true bride, the church is removed and taken to her new home prepared for her safekeeping and delight. You are in danger of expiring apart from GOD for all eternity.

Awaken and see what is about to happen to you. I cannot take you with ME if you remain stiff-necked, stubborn, and rebellious to MY Perfect Ways. Only ONE NARROW ROAD leads to Truth, MY Salvation, MY Perfect Will. Come ask ME for directions down the NARROW ROAD and I will lead you—only I can do this.

I AM THE NARROW ROAD! Few find ME—few come to know ME and few will come into MY Kingdom. Come! Be one of the few. I know MY sheep and soon I will call them out. Be ready to follow The MASTER, The SHEPHERD. Surrender your will to MINE and you will be saved!

This is your LORD and MASTER,

YAHUSHUA!

Coordinating Scripture:

Acts 9 & Acts 9:18, And immediately there fell from his eyes as it had been scales: and he received sight forthwith, and arose, and was baptized.

James 4:4, Ye adulterers and adulteresses, know ye not that the friendship of the world is enmity with GOD? Whosoever therefore will be a friend of the world is the enemy of GOD.

Matthew 7:14, Because strait is the gate, and narrow is the way, which leadeth unto life, and few there be that find it.

Word given to Susan for a reader: I received this word from the LORD for a reader and it is also a word of warning for everyone: Susan--I can give words: This is your LORD SPEAKING--I am Omnipotent, Omnipresent, Omniscient, All-Knowing, All-Powerful--Never Ending, Alpha and Omega--I come to you with love and mercy--change your ways--do it now, not later--tomorrow may be too late. This is a warning--I am sending a *HEADWIND to all the world and the people better take heed. MY bride will be removed, but the world that remains will see destruction. Avoid destruction--seek your GOD while I can still be found. Repent and get right with your GOD. Time is closing in. These Words are for your benefit. It is only by MY Power that your heart is turning to ME. Turn to ME. Now is the time. THIS is the HOLY ONE from ABOVE.

*Susan: I looked up the word headwind--as I did not know what it meant: Definition of HEADWIND: A wind that is blowing in the opposite direction the aircraft is flying, thereby impeding its forward airspeed.

*Headwind: a wind having the opposite general direction to a course of movement (as of an aircraft)

Sun, 12 May 2013

The LORD's Letter:

"If You Are Not Pursuing ME, You Are Chasing The Wind."

The Plight of the Lukewarm:

Revelation 3:16, So then because thou art lukewarm, and cold nor hot, I will spue thee out of MY Mouth.

The Lukewarm, warned of in 2 Timothy 3:4-5, they have the appearance of looking and behaving godly—they may attend church regularly but that doesn't a "Christian" make. These people are satisfied with rote religion—but GOD WANTS MORE—HE wants your ENTIRE LIFE and a relationship too. By taking your life—GOD will exchange it with HIS HOLY SPIRIT filling you and that is the power you deny if you do not give GOD your ALL that is mentioned in this scripture: 2 Timothy 3:4-5, Traitors, heady, high-minded, lovers of pleasures more than lovers of GOD: Having a form of godliness, but denying the power thereof: from such turn away.

The LORD demonstrates in 2 Peter the plight of the lukewarm church that "plays" with the things of GOD but does not make a serious stand for the LORD: 2 Peter 2:20-22, 20For if after they have escaped the pollutions of the world through the knowledge of the LORD and SAVIOR JESUS CHRIST, they are again entangled therein, and overcome, the latter end is worse with them than the beginning. 21For it had been better for them not to have known the way of righteousness, than, after they have known it, to turn from the holy commandment delivered unto them. 22But it is happened unto them according to the true proverb: The dog is turned to his own vomit again; and the sow that was washed to her wallowing in the mire.

So you either move TO GOD and give HIM everything or you are handling the things of GOD such as calling yourself a "Christian" and going through the motions of attending church, yet not really giving the LORD your ALL. Hebrews gives the warning and message of danger to those who "sample" the things of GOD and then pull back to the world:

Hebrews 10:37-39, 37For yet a little while, and HE that shall come will come, and will not tarry. 38Now the just shall live by faith: but if any man draw back, MY Soul shall have no pleasure in him. 39But we are not of them who draw back unto perdition; but of them that believe to the saving of the soul.

CHRIST addresses the lukewarm Laodicean church and says this about the lukewarm followers: Revelation 3:15, I know thy works, that thou art neither cold nor hot: I would thou wert cold or hot. CHRIST speaks to the same lukewarm group and says this according to Matthew 7:22-23, 22Many will say to ME in that day, LORD, LORD, have we not prophesied in THY Name? And in THY Name have cast out devils? And in THY Name done many wonderful works? 23And then will I profess unto them, I never knew you: depart from ME, ye that work iniquity.

Here is a picture of the lukewarm in 2 Timothy 3:7, Ever learning, and never able to come to the knowledge of the truth. And CHRIST reiterates this in Revelation 3:17, Because thou sayest, I am rich, and increased with goods, and have need of nothing; and knowest not that thou art wretched, and miserable, and poor, and blind, and naked:

The lukewarm are lost—as lost as the lost who have never received the LORD in their heart. However, the lukewarm lost are in MUCH BIGGER TROUBLE than others because they have dabbled in their faith of GOD and returned to the enemy of GOD for their future plans, answers, and devotion. It is very serious to return to the world and to reject an all-consuming pursuit of CHRIST: Hebrews 10:29, 29Of how much sorer punishment, suppose ye, shall he be thought worthy, who hath trodden underfoot the SON of GOD, and hath counted the Blood of the Covenant, wherewith he was sanctified, an unholy thing, and hath done despite unto the SPIRIT of Grace?

Now below are Letters from the LORD to you, dreams and visions, and a serious message about GOD's hatred of Santa Claus:

Words of the LORD:

"If You Are Not Pursuing ME You Are Chasing The Wind."

(Words Received from Our LORD by Susan, May 5, 2013)

Children, it is I, your LORD:

I am ready to make MY Return. I want to take MY church out of this cold, cruel world. It is getting darker by the day. The hour is coming and I want you to get ready.

The world is plummeting into deep darkness. It is choosing against ME. It desires to run apart from its GOD. I made this world, it is MY Creation. I put everything in place. I brought it all about. I am the AUTHOR and FINISHER of the Universe. Every detail is under MY Auspices.

Children, you need to run under MY Cover. You need to run under MY Blood Covering. I paid a large price so that you might have this Blood Covering. With this Blood Covering you will be found guiltless when I judge MY children. It is by the power of MY Blood that you will be saved. There is no other way. All other answers lead to destruction. You may think you have the answer, but if you are not pursuing ME you are chasing the wind.

I am the WAY, the TRUTH and the LIFE; no one comes to the FATHER except by ME. I paid a large price by MY Death on a gruesome cross. This was paid for your iniquity, your rebellion against ME, your GOD.

So now you may choose life or death. What do you choose? The world is coming to a close as you know it. Soon darkness will seep in all around you. I am taking MY bride out of this dark world. Will you be ready when I come? You must surrender your ALL to ME. Ask to be filled with MY SPIRIT. Repent of your sins before a Holy GOD. These are MY Requirements to receive MY Salvation. There is NO OTHER WAY. You have precious little time to come to terms with this Truth. These are True Words. I am not a man that I should lie.

I am GOD SUPREME,

Your LORD and your SAVIOR.

Coordinating Scriptures:

Revelation 7:14, And I said unto him, Sir, thou knowest. And he said to me, These are they which came out of great tribulation, and have washed their robes, and made them white in the blood of the LAMB.

John 14:6, JESUS saith unto him, I am the WAY, the TRUTH, and the LIFE: no man cometh unto the FATHER, but by ME.

Deuteronomy 30:19, I call heaven and earth to record this day against you, that I have set before you life and death, blessing and cursing: therefore choose life, that both thou and thy seed may live.

CHAPTER 10

Those Who Are Caught Up In The World,

Will Be Left Behind

Words of the LORD:

"Those Who Are Caught Up In The World, Will Be Left Behind."

(Words Received from Our LORD by Susan, May 7, 2013)

Daughter let us begin.

Children, it is I your LORD.

I come to you from the Heavenlies. I come to address you with MY concerns. I have a series of concerns that I want to lay before you. I am your FATHER. So few are paying attention to the things that are going on around them. So few are grasping the messages I am sending forth.

There is a wave of evil moving across the land. It is consuming the world. Few are now grasping how serious this is. If you only knew how near MY Return was, you would sit up and pay attention right now.

The trouble you see around the world is for your benefit. I am allowing the evil to move in to wake you up. Even this is not getting the attention of many. So few are stirred. So few even understand that I am at the door.

There is a time coming soon when MY children will be lifted out of the world; the ones who are paying attention and pressing into ME. Only those will be considered worthy to escape what is coming. If you do not run quickly to get under MY Cover, MY Blood Covering, you will not be considered worthy when I come to collect MY own.

Now, I want to address another issue. It is a matter of how you regard MY Holy Word. You do not want to spend any time in MY Book. You have time for everything, but MY Book. You spend hours and hours playing with the world, but never find a moment to turn to MY Book.

This is where the devil has you right where he wants you. He wants you to be found deaf, dumb and mute. MY people die from lack of knowledge. If you are in the dark, I will not find you when I come for MY own. By reading MY Word you will find the Light, the Light that lights your path. You are blinded, if you do not pursue ME through MY Word. This is where Truth can be found.

You must make time for MY Word. This can only be done by making sacrifices. Soon the Light will be taken away for those left behind. There will be very little Light left available like there is now. If you don't make time for MY Words now, you will live to regret it.

I am an Honest GOD and I must tell you the Truth. If I spare the rod, I will spoil the child. I must speak with the Rod of MY Mouth or you will be spoiled.

Children, if you are not paying attention you will be left behind. Precious few are paying attention. I will only take those who are watching and waiting on ME. These are the ones who are coming out to safety. Those who are caught up in the world, will be left behind. I am a Jealous GOD and I will not be second place. If you have other lovers besides ME, I will leave you to them.

These are serious warnings, but very few are heeding to them. As always, very few listen to MY messengers. There is nothing new under the sun. Sit up, pay attention, and get ready. MY Blood is your only SOURCE of relief!

This is your GOD: Great JEHOVAH, The "I AM"

Coordinating Scripture:

Luke 21:36, Watch ye therefore, and pray always, that ye may be accounted worthy to escape all these things that shall come to pass, and to stand before the SON of man.

Revelation 12:9-11, 9And the great dragon was cast out, that old serpent, called the devil, and satan, which deceiveth the whole world: he was cast out into the earth, and his angels were cast out with him. 10And I heard a loud voice saying in heaven, Now is come salvation, and strength, and the kingdom of our GOD, and the power of HIS CHRIST: for the accuser of our brethren is cast down, which accused them before our GOD day and night. 11And they overcame him by the Blood of the LAMB, and by the word of their testimony; and they loved not their lives unto the death.

Ephesians 5:26, That HE might sanctify and cleanse it with the washing of water by the Word,

Proverbs 13:24, He that spareth his rod hateth his son: but he that loveth him chasteneth him betimes.

Revelation 19:15, And out of HIS Mouth goeth a sharp sword, that with it HE should smite the nations: and HE shall rule them with a rod of iron: and HE treadeth the winepress of the fierceness and wrath of Almighty GOD.

Isaiah 11:1-4, And there shall come forth a ROD out of the stem of Jesse, and a BRANCH shall grow out of his roots: 2 And the SPIRIT of the LORD shall rest upon HIM, the SPIRIT of Wisdom and Understanding, the SPIRIT of Counsel and Might, the SPIRIT of Knowledge and of the fear of the LORD; 3 And shall make HIM of quick understanding in the fear of the LORD: and HE shall not judge after the sight of HIS Eyes, neither reprove after the hearing of HIS Ears: 4 But with righteousness shall HE Judge the poor, and reprove with equity for the meek of the earth: and HE shall smite the earth: with the rod of HIS Mouth, and with the breath of HIS Lips shall HE slay the wicked.

Date: Tue, 28 May 2013 00:06:35 -0700

The LORD's Words:

"I Am Coming Soon, If You Do Not See It, You Are Not Watching."

(Words Received from Our LORD by Susan, May 18, 2013)

Here are the Words of the LORD.

Today children, you must sit up and pay attention. I am going to give you serious words, more serious than usual. I am coming soon, if you do not see it, you are not watching. If you cannot see it, you are spending too much time having a love affair with the world. You are so enamored by the world that you cannot see what is happening before your eyes.

I am a GOD of Truth and I speak Truth. I am giving warnings through MY messengers that the hour is closing in and you need to

101

sit up and pay attention. Many of you will be left behind because you refuse to pay attention.

This is not the first time that I have warned MY people in the past of pending disaster. I have always given warnings. Read MY Word. You will see that MY Warnings always precede the coming disasters: for the punishments for disobedience and rebellion against GOD.

Warnings are for your benefit—they are not just to scare you. It is to keep you from falling into disaster, but you must heed MY Warnings to keep yourself from disaster. Today is no different. I am warning you to prepare yourself to be ready, to be rescued from the coming disaster.

You must surrender your life to ME FULLY, including your hopes and future plans. I want ALL of you. If you do not do this you still belong to MY enemy. You are his and you do his will. Come to ME in FULL surrender; apply the covering of MY Precious Blood; wash your mind, hands and feet with MY Words; repent of your sin and rebellion against ME; forgive ALL so I can forgive you. Come to ME and receive a filling of MY HOLY SPIRIT. Come ask to have your oil lamps filled by MY SPIRIT.

These are MY Terms. I want to include you among the number I take out to safety when I come for MY bride. Will you be in attendance at MY Marriage Supper? This is your Official Invitation. Let others know they are also invited. I await your response. I extend MY Hand to you in marriage.

This is your LORD and SAVIOR.

Coordinating Scripture:

Jeremiah 6:10, To whom shall I speak, and give warning, that they may hear? Behold, their ear is uncircumcised, and they cannot hearken: behold, the Word of the LORD is unto them a reproach; they have no delight in it.

Revelation 1:5, And from JESUS CHRIST, WHO is the FAITHFUL WITNESS, and the FIRST BEGOTTEN of the dead, and the PRINCE of the kings of the earth. Unto HIM that loved us, and washed us from our sins in HIS Own Blood,

Job 9:30, If I wash myself with snow water, and make my hands never so clean;

Hebrews 10:22, Let us draw near with a true heart in full assurance of faith, having our hearts sprinkled from an evil conscience, and our bodies washed with pure water.

Ephesians 5:26, That HE might sanctify and cleanse it with the washing of water by the word,

Ephesians 6:15, And your feet shod with the preparation of the gospel of peace;

Words of the LORD:

"I Am Ready To Pour Down MY SPIRIT Over MY People Like FIRE."

(Words Received from Our LORD by Susan, May 19, 2013)

WE can begin: MY children this is your GOD Speaking. I have words that I want to convey to you.

I am ready to come like a whirlwind over MY people. I am ready to pour down MY SPIRIT over MY people like FIRE. I want MY children to open themselves up to the move of MY SPIRIT.

These are the last days. The end is coming, as you know it. The world has enjoyed the Grace of GOD. It has seen Great Mercy poured down from MY Throne. I am however, disappointed: the world is turning its back to its GOD. The world is moving against its GOD. The world is showing little respect to ME, its MAKER. I created everyone and everything in it and yet MY children have become rebellious. They are moving against MY Words and MY Ways. The evil one is glorified in their hearts. They have lifted up the enemy in their hearts. He has dethroned ME in their hearts. I am no longer first place to the children I created.

This brings ME to great sadness. Your GOD is weeping and crying. I am full of sadness: that MY children have turned their backs to ME. I am sad for them and for MYSELF. I will soon remove the few: who still hold ME dear in their hearts. There are a handful on earth who still pursue ME with all their heart. Very few look to ME for all their answers. Most have turned away from ME and pursue their answers from the world.

There is only a brief time remaining. You must turn your heart back to ME. MY Hands are outstretched to receive you. I am willing to take you back into MY Arms. I am willing to hold you and save you. Come to ME in full surrender; lay your life down at MY Feet; give ME your ALL, repent of your sin that comes between us; let MY SPIRIT guide you; ask for HIM to fill you. MY SON, MYSELF your FATHER, and MY SPIRIT: WE join the bride and WE say, "Come." Come to the glories that I have in store for you when I remove MY church. This is all waiting for you. I say, "Come."

This is your FATHER, GOD ALMIGHTY, the BEGINING, the END, ALPHA and OMEGA.

That is good enough.

Coordinating Scriptures:

Nahum 1:3, The LORD is slow to anger, and great in power, and will not at all acquit the wicked: the LORD hath HIS way in the whirlwind and in the storm, and the clouds are the dust of HIS Feet.

Psalm 20:7, Some trust in chariots, and some in horses: but we will remember the Name of the LORD our GOD.

CHAPTER 11

The LORD's Words:

"I am coming. I spoke it and I will fulfill it!"

Mon, 17 Jun 2013

The LORD's Words: "I am coming. I spoke it and I will fulfill it!"

We live in a "pick and choose" world. That is the way many Christians view the Bible: "pick and choose" from the Bible what you want to believe. For instance, a "pick and choose" belief is the one in which people want to believe that once they are saved they are always saved regardless of their life style. This was a doctrine formulated by the enemy for the purpose of tripping up people from making it to Heaven. "Once saved, always saved" is a fabulous doctrine for those who love the world and want to be caught up in it but we know that GOD says the world is an ENMITY to HIM and so is the idea that someone can receive eternal salvation and cannot possibly lose it over the course of their life regardless of their behavior and attitude toward GOD.

The Bible is full of scripture that CONTRADICTS the belief that once you are saved you can never: be entangled again in the pollutions of the world that you have escaped...fall away...be moved away from the hope of the gospel...be castaway...put CHRIST to an open shame. Here is reference scripture:

2 Peter 2:20 (KJV): For if after they have escaped the pollutions of the world through the knowledge of the LORD and SAVIOR CHRIST, they are again entangled therein, and overcome, the latter end is worse with them than the beginning.

Hebrews 6:4-6 (KJV): 4 For it is impossible for those who were once enlightened, and have tasted of the heavenly gift, and were made partakers of the HOLY GHOST, 5 And have tasted the good Word of GOD, and the powers of the world to come, 6 If they shall fall away, to renew them again unto repentance; seeing they crucify to themselves the SON of GOD afresh, and put HIM to an open shame.

Colossians 1:23 (KJV): If ye continue in the faith grounded and settled, and be not moved away from the hope of the gospel, which ye have heard, and which was preached to every creature which is under heaven; whereof I Paul am made a minister;

1 Corinthians 9:26-27 (KJV): 26I therefore so run, not as uncertainly; so fight I, not as one that beateth the air: 27 But I keep under my body, and bring it into subjection: lest that by any means, when I have preached to others, I myself should be a castaway.

1 Peter 4:18 (KJV): And if the righteous scarcely be saved, where shall the ungodly and the sinner appear?

Another "pick and choose" doctrine of deceit is the idea that the baptism of the HOLY SPIRIT is a "works" doctrine. In reality, attempting to live out the Christian life apart from the baptism and indwelling of the HOLY SPIRIT in the individual IS the TRUE "works" doctrine. You are engaging in "works" if you are attempting to live by the Law of GOD without the baptism of the HOLY SPIRIT (the moment someone invites the HOLY SPIRIT to come into their life to replace "self" with the HOLY SPIRIT with the person's spirit). Apart from the individual receiving the baptism of the HOLY SPIRIT by asking for it, he performs the law by his own power outside of the supernatural Power of the HOLY SPIRIT indwelling the SPIRIT-filled person. It is the HOLY SPIRIT—WHO is in a fully-surrendered person and WHO then can guide someone to successfully follow the Laws GOD gave for mankind to follow and live by.

Here are scriptures that testify to the individual's need to persevere or endure trials which sounds like a form of "works" but is really the requirement of GOD to persevere and overcome trials to reach the goal ultimately to salvation. Let the scriptures speak for themselves:

James 1:12 (KJV): Blessed is the man that endureth temptation: for when he is tried, he shall receive the crown of life, which the LORD hath promised to them that love HIM.

Ephesians 6:18 (KJV): Praying always with all prayer and supplication in the SPIRIT, and watching thereunto with all perseverance and supplication for all saints;

Revelation 2:3 (KJV): And hast borne, and hast patience, and for MY Name's sake hast laboured, and hast not fainted.

Words of the LORD:

"If you are caught up in 'sudden destruction' apart from ME and MY Rapture you will go to hell."

(Words Received from Our LORD by Susan, May 29, 2013)

I am ready to give you Words. The hour is approaching for MY Return. I am near, even at the door. Children, you act as if this event will never happen. You act as if MY Coming is a spoof or a joke. You act as if your GOD does not exist and MY Words are not good. You treat ME as if I am a liar and the signs that I put out are all being ignored.

The signs are for your benefit. I gave signs so that you can know to be ready. This is all for your benefit. I know when I am coming. I know the day of MY arrival. I know the day I will be approaching for the church. You, on the other hand, need to watch for the signs. This is MY Gift, MY Warning for all those who watch, to pay attention. This is for those who want to be ready at MY Coming, for those who desire to be ready when I come for the church.

I could have come without warning but this is not MY Way. I want the people to know I care enough to give them warning, that I love them enough to give them time to prepare. Without this warning most of you would be lost. As it is, with the warning, most are still not paying attention. The only thing left now is for MY Coming. I can come at any moment but most of you are not watching and you will be left behind or lost in the coming sudden destruction.

If you are caught up in "sudden destruction" apart from ME and MY Rapture you will go to hell. If you doubt this, read MY Word. MY Word is clear. If you spend time in MY Word you will see that the signs that I put forth are now happening in the world. I have not misled anyone. It has all been laid out before you.

Make your preparations now to be ready for MY Coming. Don't be deceived by someone who tells you something different. Take time and read MY Word for yourself. Dig deep into MY Word, get to know ME for yourself. Come to ME for a personal relationship. Don't just take the word of others that I am not coming soon. Learn the Truth for yourself. You will be held accountable when you face ME someday, you alone. Get to know your GOD. Don't waste another moment.

FATHER GOD, (YAHUSHUA's FATHER).

Coordinating Scripture:

Jude 1:18 (KJV): How that they told you there should be mockers in the last time, who should walk after their own ungodly lusts.

2 Timothy 4:8 (KJV): Henceforth there is laid up for me a crown of righteousness, which the LORD, the RIGHTEOUS JUDGE, shall give me at that day: and not to me only, but unto all them also that love HIS appearing.

1 Thessalonians 5:3 (KJV): For when they shall say, Peace and safety; then sudden destruction cometh upon them, as travail upon a woman with child; and they shall not escape.

Romans 14:12 (KJV): So then every one of us shall give account of himself to GOD.

Words of the LORD:

"It is I, your LORD. I am coming. I spoke it and I will fulfill it! It is MY Word—MY Word never fails."

(Words Received from Our LORD by Susan, May 31, 2013)

Yes, I can give you Words:

It is I, your LORD. I am coming. I spoke it and I will fulfill it! It is MY Word—MY Word never fails.

The hour is approaching for this fulfillment. You will continue to see events leading up to this event: things spoken of so long ago. These events will intensify as MY Coming is close.

Don't let MY Coming take you by surprise. Let these signs speak to your spirit: wake you up. I do not want you to be paralyzed with fear, but I do want you to have a healthy fear of GOD. Don't fall asleep at the wheel when I come for MY own. Many will be caught unawares—but not caught up to safety: horror and terror will be their reward for not paying attention and for not watching and seeking ME for MY Salvation and Guidance.

This hour approaches and the majority cannot focus on their GOD. The world is just too enticing. Soon the enticement of the world will go flat: the flavor will be a bitter pill to swallow.

Seek your GOD. Surrender your all to ME. I am worth knowing. I bled and died for you. I gave you life and your being. Come to know ME today. It is almost time for these events to take place. Hide under MY Wing. Come under MY Blood Covering. There is no other place to retreat...

I am the SHELTER in a STORM—I AM.

Coordinating Scripture:

1 King 8:56: There hath not failed one Word of all HIS Good Promise.

Psalm 119:89: Forever, O LORD, THY Word is settled in Heaven.

Psalm 119:160: Every one of THY Judgements endureth forever.

Isaiah 40:8: The Word of GOD shall stand forever.

Isaiah 55:10, 11: So shall MY Word be...it shall accomplish...and prosper.

Matthew 24:35: Heaven and earth shall pass away, but MY Words never.

John 10:35: The Scripture cannot be broken (cancelled, annulled).

1 Peter 1:25: The Word of the LORD endureth forever.

CHAPTER 12

"How to Hear the Voice of GOD"

by Donna McDonald

End Times Prophecy Conference Presentation

"How to Hear the Voice of GOD" given by Donna McDonald:

June 8, 2013

My dear friends, my old friends and my new friends:

These words were dictated to me from the LORD. You see, I am not a public speaker, I am a servant. The LORD speaks and I am to obey. First of all I want to repent of my sins before a HOLY GOD, I cast out the enemy and send him to hell under the precious Name of YAHUSHUA, I cover this room, myself, and all the attendees with the precious blood of YAHUSHUA. I protect this area under the Holy Name of the LORD.

I pray to the LORD and I give HIM myself, I give HIM my arms, my legs, my body, my heart, my mind, my spirit. I give HIM everything. I tell HIM I want all of HIM and want to go deeper with HIM. Well, if you give HIM all of yourself and tell HIM you want more of HIM-all of HIM, something is going to happen. I received the gift of hearing HIS Voice almost two years ago. HE has revealed amazing things to me ever since.

I want to tell you how I received this letter from the LORD. I was in the car with my kids in the back seat and my husband driving and we were going down the highway at 65 mph on the way to Florida. My son, Austin, set up my computer so it would act as a word processor. I said to the LORD that I was ready to hear a message from the HOLY SPIRIT about what I should say at the conference. HE spoke these words to me to share with you. I typed as I heard HIM speak. My family can attest to this. I read them the words as soon as I was finished typing them.

This is what HE wants to say to you. I have prayed and received these words and HE is speaking these words prophetically to you:

I created the stars in the sky and the sand on the beaches. I created birds and butterflies and leaves and trees. I have created mountains and oceans and lakes and paths and streams. I have created everything beautiful for you to enjoy. I created it all for you, MY children, to enjoy while you are firmly planted on this earth. I have also created the heavens for you to enjoy. All of you have had your feet firmly planted on this earth but not all of MY creation will see heaven.

They will stand at the gates of heaven and will meet ME Eye to eye some day, one day, but not all will hear, "Well done good and faithful servant." Only those who give ME their all will hear those Words. Only those who put aside ALL of their own hopes, plans, and dreams will ever see MY Home, the one MY FATHER created for ME and the one I have created for you. Only those children who place ME first in their lives will ever see ME Face to face and will enter heaven where I have created great places for you to enjoy.

It is not enough that you go to church, drive your mother to the store, read MY Bible occasionally or call out to ME in your time of need. No one's religion or their church traditions or their statues or idols ever saved them, nor their rote prayers. I want MY children to call out to ME everyday in prayer. I want MY children to look on ME as their BEST FRIEND, to treat ME like I am the BEST THING that ever happened to them. When I died on the cross, a horrible death, I

114

became the BEST THING that ever happened to each one of you. I broke the curse once and for all over sin and over religion and all the do's and don'ts that the prior generation knew.

MY FATHER gave ME for you so that you would not have to suffer and endure the torture and pain that I did when I died for you on the cross: a feat that no man has ever endured and lived through like I did until I died late in the afternoon that day at Golgotha. I became the perfect sacrifice for you. I became your LAMB on that cold, cruel cross to suffer for you so that you would not have to. Why would MY children want to take 'matters,' in their own lives, into their own hands, instead of putting their lives into MY Capable GODLY Hands? Why would you think you know what is best for yourself when I know all and I have created all and I know the perfect plan for you?

Run from all evil. Run into MY Arms. The world that I created for you is dying and decaying little by little. It is a stench to MY FATHER. HE can hardly tolerate it anymore. HE is ready to take MY bride out and throw a big party for ME in Heaven. You are all invited. Just make sure you get there. You must "RSVP" by submitting your life and everything you love and enjoy and look forward to, to ME. Submit your ALL to ME.

I will tell you now, how you can hear MY Voice. You do not need to read a book, though you may want to. MY son, Dr. Virkler, has written a book called "Dialogue with GOD" to assist you in hearing MY Voice. MY Words here are all you need. This is what you need to do:

1. Submit yourself to ME: your GOD. Live for ME. Do not plan ahead: just listen to ME and I will guide and direct your paths.

2. Quiet yourself and listen to what I have to say to you.

3. Focus on ME. Picture yourself sitting on a park bench or pleasant location looking at ME and conversing with ME. The picture MY daughter, Akiane, drew is the most correct picture of ME ever known on the earth. Look up MY picture on the internet so you will know WHO you are talking to.

4. Pray and ask for forgiveness of your sins before a HOLY GOD. Ask ME if there is anything I want to say to you. Then clear your mind and just listen for ME to speak.

5. I am a gentleman. I am a Patient and Humble GOD. I have needs and I have desires and I desire to be number ONE in your life. Most people do not think that I have needs, because I am their GOD, but I do have needs and I created you to meet MY needs.

6. I have a need for love and affection. I have a need to be given attention. I have a need for praise and worship and I have a need to hear YOUR VOICE. You want to hear MY VOICE: well, I want to hear YOUR VOICE as well.

When you submit to ME, quiet yourself, pray and repent and listen. You will hear MY Voice. I may not speak where you can listen right away, but I will eventually. Keep talking and listening and I will eventually respond to you. I respond verbally with a Still, Small Voice and also I respond by showing MYSELF to you. I show MYSELF everytime you hear a baby cry, or see a majestic mountain, or a perfectly blue sky, a rainbow, a sunny sky peeking through the clouds, a field full of wildflowers or a doe and her fawn by the side of the road. I share these beautiful creations for all to see. No one can say they never knew there was a GOD. Even those deep in the rainforests of Africa can say they have seen their GOD in the beauty of created nature.

Pursue ME as your only hope, for I AM YOUR ONLY HOPE in this dark, dark world. Every moment the world is getting darker and is spiraling down. Only those who pursue ME one hundred percent and give ME their entire life and all their hopes, plans, and dreams will make it off this planet alive and well. Do not be those unwise children who choose darkness by not giving ME their one hundred percent. The world is getting more and more evil. The antichrist spirit is rising up as WE speak and breathe here. Choose for ME and Choose for Life: for I Am the WAY, the TRUTH, and the LIFE. No one comes to the FATHER except through ME.

The end, daughter: signed, sealed and delivered with a kiss.

Donna McDonald 5/21/13

CHAPTER 13

Humble Hearts Will Walk With Their GOD

Mon, 1 Jul 2013

This is the hour of repentance, weeping and wailing...

John: 8:44: Ye are of your father the devil, and the lusts of your father ye will do. He was a murderer from the beginning, and abode not in the truth, because there is no truth in him. When he speaketh a lie, he speaketh of his own: for he is a liar, and the father of it.

Matthew 7:21: Not everyone that saith unto ME, LORD, LORD, shall enter into the kingdom of heaven; but he that doeth the Will of MY FATHER which is in heaven.

These scriptures show that there are only two wills: GOD's or satan's. So the question for you is your will following the enemy of GOD or GOD?

I point this scripture out because of something the LORD revealed to me recently for the purpose of sharing with others: If you do not belong to GOD because you are not fully sold out to HIM and completely dead to "self" and surrendering your ALL to GOD then you still are in the hands of the enemy, to be used by him however he chooses. This is of course, is something very few people seem to be aware of because if they were aware—there would be more people deciding to surrender their ALL over to CHRIST.

When your spirit is not of GOD and it is the enemy's, all the enemy wants is to destroy you. Although it does not seem possible, the enemy will have free access to your life to do his will and use your life for his evil plans. Many people have evil spirits who want them to be destroyed through: divorce; loss of income; loss of life, and cast into hell ultimately. The Bible gives an example of how spirits inside someone can lead them into life- and soul-threatening situations—like this young boy who was doing things he did not want to do:

Matthew 17:14-18: 14And when they were come to the multitude, there came to him a certain man, kneeling down to him, and saying, 15LORD, have mercy on my son: for he is lunatic, and sore vexed: for oft times he falleth into the fire, and oft into the water. 1And I brought him to THY disciples, and they could not cure him. 17Then JESUS answered and said, O faithless and perverse generation, how long shall I be with you? How long shall I suffer you? Bring him hither to ME. 18And JESUS rebuked the devil; and he departed out of him: and the child was cured from that very hour.

Just like this scripture above describes the evil spirit and the devil ruling over the child causing him to fall into the fire and into the water, imagine that satan, who wants you to fail is actually trying to lead you to do the things that would destroy you and your eternal life—causing you to fall into the fire and into the water. Stop falling into the fires and deep waters the enemy wants to drag you in and out of. Be free of this evil—Surrender your ALL to CHRIST and choose GOD's Perfect Will over your own will.

Just a few news notes on our ministry work:

"Marriage Supper of the Lamb" and "Rapture and Tribulation" Books Now on iTunes:

Hello fans of "Marriage Supper of the Lamb" and other Susan Davis books, I want to let you know that they are now published on iTunes, available for free. This means that you can read her books

119

on your iPhone, iPod Touch, or iPad. Make sure you download the iBooks app from the App Store and then search for either Susan Davis' name or the book titles below in the search box. Below is the link to these books. "Left Behind After the Rapture" and others are still being processed through Apple's quality control. Tell others who may have an Apple Device to download it as well. God Bless.

"MARRIAGE SUPPER OF THE LAMB"

https://itunes.apple.com/us/book/marriage-supper-lamb/id651680028?ls=1

"RAPTURE OR TRIBULATION"

https://itunes.apple.com/us/book/rapture-or-tribulation/id655867064?mt=11

"Humble hearts will walk with their GOD."

Words Received from Our LORD by Susan, June 22, 2013

Susan, this is your GOD—I am ready to give you Words:

The hour is approaching of MY Return for the church. It closes in. Each day, I draw nearer. The Season is now! You are in the season to be watching closely. This is not the time to be sitting on your hands or closing your eyes. This is the time to be vigilant. Keep your nose pressed to the glass—watching, looking, listening for MY Trumpet Blast.

I will come like a thief in the night. If you are not watching, you will not be taken when I come back to rescue MY church, to bring out MY bride. She is gathering under MY Mantle: MY Blood Covering. I only have eyes for her—for MY bride: those who choose to follow

ME, their GOD and to lay down their affection for the world and all it stands for.

MY bride has no taste for the world and its false attraction. Many have turned to the world for all their answers, hoping to receive truth for life's problems through men and MY enemy's works. He has always longed to lead men astray and only wants to deceive mankind and take MY children to hell. This is what happens, when MY children are asleep and not watching. They are deceived and easily fall into enemy hands.

Deception is running high now and the only way to discern Truth is by surrendering your life over to ME with a humble submission: pressing in to your GOD; receiving MY Blood Covering and Salvation that I earned for you by hanging on a cross with a brutal death. I willingly surrender MY ALL to die for you in your place, to cover your sins committed against a HOLY GOD, your FATHER, WHO has established Laws to live by.

Your sin is rebellion before your GOD, your CREATOR. All have sinned and fallen short of the Glory of GOD. Now, because of the awesome price I paid, I can buy back your Salvation: pay your penalty for your lifetime of sinful acts: treason against a HOLY GOD. Now, you can rest assured that your salvation is secured and you can spend eternity with your GOD instead of being cast away from MY Presence into eternal hell—punishment for your evil life.

Take freely MY Salvation and MY SPIRIT will come live in your spirit so that you can live sin-free by the Power of the HOLY SPIRIT, but you must first surrender your ALL. Give ME ALL of you and I will give you all of ME: MY Salvation and MY SPIRIT to reside within your heart to lead you, instruct you, comfort you, and assist you in life's difficult moments.

Come! Live life in all its fullness by the Power of MY HOLY SPIRIT. You decide: do you want to live your true destiny and the plan I have written for your life: MY Will for your life? Come into MY Saving Grace and Power to fight sin, expose evil, and bring you back to MY Kingdom on earth and in heaven. You will be ready to take flight when I come to retrieve MY bride.

Now is the time to make this exchange: your sin-filled life for MY Beautiful and perfect plans for you—plans I have penned long ago for you to walk in and live in peace to commune with your GOD and MAKER. Come get right with your GOD. Don't delay. Surrender your ALL.

Humble hearts will walk with their GOD. Only these will ever know ME, truly know ME. Humility is the narrow road. Come to MY Grace and Love everlasting.

I am the KING of kings,

LORD of lords,

HUMBLE GOD.

Coordinating Scriptures:

1 Thessalonians 5:1-2: 5But of the times and the seasons, brethren, ye have no need that I write unto you. 2 For yourselves know perfectly that the Day of the LORD so cometh as a thief in the night.

Matthew 24:31: 31 And HE shall send HIS angels with a great sound of a trumpet, and they shall gather together HIS elect from the four winds, from one end of heaven to the other.

1 John 2:15: Love not the world, neither the things that are in the world. If any man love the world, the love of the FATHER is not in him.

Jeremiah 29:11: For I know the thoughts that I think toward you, saith the LORD, thoughts of peace, and not of evil, to give you an expected end.

Psalm 37:23: The steps of a good man are ordered by the LORD: and HE delighteth in his way.

CHAPTER 14

This Is The Hour Of Repentance, Weeping, Wailing ...

Words of the LORD:

"This is the hour of repentance, weeping and wailing over your sinfulness."

Words Received from Our LORD by Susan, June 23, 2013

Susan, it is I, your GOD. I am ready to begin. These words are for whoever will listen and for whoever has a heart for their GOD:

Children of the MOST HIGH, I am asking you to repent before a HOLY GOD. This is the hour of repentance, weeping and wailing over your sinfulness, over your lust for the world, your lusting eyes for the world. You have put another god before ME, many gods, actually. You have placed ME at the bottom of your list. You have dishonored ME because you love the world more than ME. I am not at the top of the mind.

I am not the first thought in the morning or the last thought at night. Many of you spend very little time with ME throughout your days. You make lots of time for many other pursuits. You find many worldly activities more important than your pursuit of ME, your GOD. You make other people, other activities and other pursuits of greater worthiness to you than ME, your MAKER. Why do you think that is so?

You have clearly made up your mind to take the low road than to pursue the high road. The high road is a very narrow road. Very few will make their way to this very narrow road. The world will pull you away as you try to make your way down MY narrow road. The

124

enemy will clutch and pull the people off the narrow road that leads to MY Salvation, MY Truth, and ultimately MY Kingdom where MY true followers come for eternity. You must set your sights on this narrow path. You must seek ME in all your ways. You must surrender your all to ME, your GOD, and I do mean your ALL.

I cannot accept a partial filling of your lamp oil: a partial relationship will not do. If you believe yourself ready to come with ME in MY Rapture, then you would have thrown off the world completely. You would have walked away from your own will, laid yourself before ME in repentance and begged to be in MY Perfect Will at all costs. Anything else puts you in danger of eternal failure: a failure to be saved and failing to be with GOD for eternity.

These words are sincere, they are serious. You must take them seriously if you want to be saved. Half-hearted love for GOD is as good as outright hatred of GOD. You either love ME, MY Will, and MY Ways or you reject ME. There is no middle ground.

Now decide for yourself: will you be with ME in My Kingdom for eternity or will you die in your sin apart from your GOD cast into eternal hell? Choices must be made—these are your choices to make: no one else's. Don't be deceived there is no other way. Come into MY Glorious Light, receive salvation, choose for ME, surrender your all to ME, repent of your ugly sin, and then come live in MY Will for your life.

These words are for your benefit. The time is short, come quickly and find your GOD. Cast your cares on ME. I will bear your burdens. I await your answer.

This is your GOD ALMIGHTY,

The LOVER of your soul.

Coordinating Scripture:

James 4:4: Ye adulterers and adulteresses, know ye not that the friendship of the world is enmity with GOD? Whosoever therefore will be a friend of the world is the enemy of GOD.

Galatians 5:16-17: 16This I say then, Walk in the SPIRIT, and ye shall not fulfil the lust of the flesh. 17For the flesh lusteth against the SPIRIT, and the SPIRIT against the flesh: and these are contrary the one to the other: so that ye cannot do the things that ye would.

Matthew 25:4: 4 But the wise took oil in their vessels with their lamps.

Matthew 7:14: Because strait is the gate, and narrow is the way, which leadeth unto life, and few there be that find it.

1 Peter 5:7: Casting all your care upon HIM; for HE careth for you.

Prepare for the very soon rapture.

Read all the books by Susan Davis :

Bride of Christ – Prepare Now !

Left Behind After The Rapture

Rapture or Tribulation

Marriage Supper of the Lamb

Also by Susan Davis and Sabrina De Muynck

I Am Coming, Volume 1

I Am Coming, Volume 2

I Am Coming, Volume 3

I Am Coming, Volume 4

I Am Coming, Volume 5

I Am Coming, Volume 6

Available as paperbacks and kindle ebooks at:
www.amazon.com

Also available for free as ebooks (various formats) at:
www.smashwords.com

Made in USA - Kendallville, IN
1146769_9781490519029
08.11.2020 0752